Jump
or Die

WRITTEN BY
DOUGLAS JENNINGS

First Published in Great Britain in 2005 by
Tucann Books

ISBN N° 1 873257 50 3

Produced by: TUCANN*design&print*, 19 High Street,
Heighington Lincoln LN4 1RG
Tel & Fax: 01522 790009
www.tucann.co.uk

Colfe's Grammar School

The afternoon sun shone brightly through the windows of the classroom and the quiet hum and murmur of the school at work had a soporific effect on the English lesson in progress for Upper 5c. The form were reading aloud, one by one, from their books, a device to keep them all occupied for School Certificate examinations were finished and the end of term was in sight. Results would be published during the summer holiday, all was peaceful.

The calm was shattered by ,my frantic shout as the wasp that had descended from its nest in the eaves arrived at my shoulder via the inside of my coat sleeve. My efforts to shake it free resulted in several more stings, more cries of pain and a chance for the rest of the class to add to the din by stamping feet and banging desk lids. Detention and the cane, however, backed discipline in those days, so order was soon restored. I was despatched for first aid and the reading resumed - it was Summer 1939 and I was 17.

The examination results. School Certificate, as it was known, were published in August and necessitated a special journey to the school to find the list posted up in the lobby. The school seemed quiet and lifeless, without the tramp and scurry of the boys, they were never to return, evacuated during the month to Tunbridge Wells where they shared another school, (Skinners) and the building devastated by bombs and a flying bomb a few years hence. So ended the 'School on the Hill' in Lewisham South East London'.

Colfe's was rebuilt after the War, however, on their playing fields at Eltham and continues its distinguished history.

When I found my name on the results list it was with some relief that I had qualified for two extra years and would then have the chance of a place at a University, providing I passed yet another exam. The new term did not start until the middle of September in Tunbridge Wells but events were moving against me and at home the signs of the coming war had arrived in the back garden. The Anderson shelter consisted of sections

Colfe's Grammar School, Cricket 4th 11 1939 - Douglas Jennings second from left on thre front row Back Row: HV Dacombe Esq, AT Witney, ED Price, HDP Birkby, LR Lucas, DH Hider, GG Samuel (Scorer) Front Row: VF Gold, DA Jennings, REJ Locke (Capt) RB Ellis, EL Stokes

of shaped corrugated iron bolted together and sunk into the ground with the excavated soil on top and around the sides. Entrance was through a small opening in the front, which was covered on the inside with a thick curtain for blackout purposes. My eldest brother rigged up a switch and light ran from a battery, my help in digging out the hole and generally obstructing my two brothers was not really appreciated. They did a good job, five years later it withstood the blast of a V.1. dropping 30 yards away. My Father died in 1934 and my Mother and I, with my two brothers lived in Catford, a South Eastern suburb of London.

When Neville Chamberlain declared war on Sunday September 3rd, we expected the immediate air raid warning that followed the announcement at 11a.m. A false alarm it may have been, but we were at least prepared complete with gas masks - not exactly in the shelter, which still had a foot of water in it, but stood nearby, ready for the holocaust. The phoney war, as it was known, lasted from September 1939 to May 1940; during this time one of my bothers was called up and joined the Army, the other was deemed too old at 41 (he had been a pilot in 1918). I had rejoined the school in Tunbridge Wells, but trying to study in "evacuee" conditions had proved hopeless, and I took a job as a junior clerk with a Life Assurance Company for the princely salary of £90 - per annum!

4

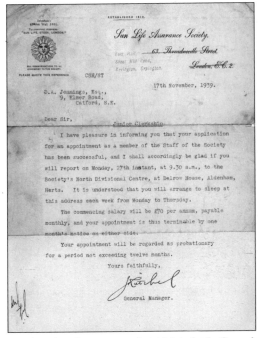

ESTABLISHED 1810.

Sun Life Assurance Society.

East Hull, 63, Threadneedle Street,
Sheet Hill Road,
Kensington, Orpington.
London, E.C. 2.

CSH/ST

17th November, 1939.

D.A. Jennings, Esq.,
9, Elmer Road,
Catford, S.E.

Dear Sir,
        Junior Clerkship.

    I have pleasure in informing you that your application
for an appointment as a member of the Staff of the Society
has been successful, and I shall accordingly be glad if you
will report on Monday, 27th instant, at 9.30 a.m., to the
Society's North Divisional Centre, at Delrow House, Aldenham,
Herts.   It is understood that you will arrange to sleep at
this address each week from Monday to Thursday.

    The commencing salary will be £70 per annum, payable
monthly, and your appointment is thus terminable by one
month's notice on either side.

    Your appointment will be regarded as probationary
for a period not exceeding twelve months.

                Yours faithfully,

                General Manager.

Very formal notification - note the initials befor the General Manager signs and the salary!

The Head Office of the Company had been moved out of Central London to a country mansion with extensive grounds and stables. The latter had been converted into living accommodation and there I lodged along with a few other young men, only returning home at weekends. The house was situated 5 miles from Watford, we ate at a local restaurant and one of our number had a sports car which meant that we could visit the bright lights occasionally. Not that these amounted to much in the blackout, a visit to the cinema or pub, or even a call at the cafe on the adjacent by-pass for exotic beans on toast. We would willingly have shared these delights with the girls who worked as typists in the office, but most of them, who lived locally, were more interested in the Army Officers stationed in the area.' Keeping up Morale,' I think it was called. Later in the war they were called up and I came across one of them as a W.A.A.F. corporal in the mapping section.

During these winter into spring months, 1939/1940, the daily war communiqués were short and quoted limited action on the Western Front.

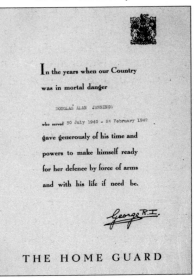

In the years when our Country was in mortal danger

DOUGLAS ALAN JENNINGS

who served 30 July 1940 - 24 February 1942 gave generously of his time and powers to make himself ready for her defence by force of arms and with his life if need be.

George R.I.

THE HOME GUARD

No medals - just a certificate. Most of the older men had 1914-1918 medals referred to as Pip, Squeak and Wilfred

Popular songs of the time were "Roll out the barrel" and "We're gonna hang out the washing on the Siegfried Line", the latter fading away as the Germans swept all before them in May 1940, and the war came nearer every day. In June came Dunkirk, and with it a mood of the people of this country, which was elated by the success of the evacuation of the troops, inspired by Churchill's stirring speeches and at the same time one of grim determination to defend the country by all means possible. Much has been written since, about how easy it would have been for the German troops if they had invaded England. I am sure that the phrase "take one with you" would have been reality, so determined and resolute was the population at that time. The country was united as never before, or since for that matter.

The call to form a "Local Defence Volunteer" force, or L. D. V. as they were first named, was overwhelmed with men, mostly veterans from the 1914-18 war, and young men awaiting call up. We made up a unit at the office, were issued with L.D.V. arm bands and drilled with broomsticks, complete with brush heads , as rifles, which caused some hilarity. when we came to presenting arms. The uniforms we were issued with at first, were Khaki overalls which fitted where they touched, later on we had the ordinary serge uniforms complete with leather gaiters. Weapons of any kind were very scarce (some units were issued with pikes) , main offensive weapons were "Molotov cocktails" - bottles filled with petrol with a rag stuffed in the top. (For use, ignite the rag, throw the bottle at the target; on impact the petrol should spray out and catch fire). Our tactical disposition was from behind a wall, which ran alongside the road near our mansion/ office, the idea to launch the bottle on to passing enemy reconnaissance troops. How long they would have stood for that is debatable, and Look, Duck and Vanish was not just a joke!

The Germans chose not to try us out, and the L.D.V. became the Home Guard and we got better equipment and better trained every month. On one weekend visit to my home in South East London I saw the start of the German attack on London. From a vantage point beside the air raid shelter I could see the mass of high flying aircraft moving slowly across the blue sky, small silvery shapes with even smaller specks darting between them. Above the steady drone of the engines one could hear rattling sounds from the fighters' guns and deeper howling noises as the fighters dived in and out of the oncoming mass. The bombers were heading for the docks some 10 miles away and in daylight they could not miss; after they had gone and darkness fell, the whole of our part of London reflected the glow of the fires.

More daylight raids followed, many driven off before they reached London, the barrage balloons ensured that they were mostly high level attacks and the newspapers reported aircraft losses like cricket scores - Luftwaffe 142 RAF 33 for 5 pilots saved. Figures for losses quoted at the time were later found inaccurate or even impossible, but once again the mood of the people was one of defiance and the question most often asked "How many today"?

In mid-September at 188 reported losses in a single day, the Luftwaffe had had enough of daylight raids and turned to night bombing of London, introducing the "Blitzkrieg" or "Blitz". Raids started at dusk and lasted spasmodically most of the night, every night for some months. Near Watford where I was working during the week it was very noisy but tolerable, at weekends whilst I was at home it meant sleeping in the air raid shelter. To get home I had to travel after work from Watford into Central London and change on to the Southern Railway to Catford. This meant that I was crossing London at the start of the nightly 'Blitz'. Although the trains were blacked out there was usually a series of flashes and thumps going on, but my fellow passengers just got on with reading their papers in the dim blue lights or dozed, the Luftwaffe were just a nuisance to be ignored!

On the return journey in daylight the damage was revealed with piles of rubble, bomb craters and fire hoses littering the streets, but again the commuters picked their way through the debris, no problem, just going to work. It must have been disconcerting for many to find when they got there that their workplace no longer existed!

Despite the noisy anti-aircraft fire, which often sounded like a pile of tin trays being dropped, we slept soundly, getting accustomed to swishes, thuds and bangs. One morning we climbed out of the shelter to find a bomb had demolished a house not 100 yards away; we had slept through the explosion! Possibly we were semi-comatose from the lack of air, three of us in a small shelter, certainly the condensation ran down the corrugated iron walls in rivers.

My eldest brother's place of work was demolished by a land mine and he joined me working near Watford so we moved house early 1941 to Pinner in Middlesex. This brought a relief from bombing noises and being near Northolt gave us the chance to see great waves of RAF fighters going out for sweeps over the Channel and Northern France.

I transferred from my office platoon in the Home Guard to a local unit at Pinner. Most of the men were 1914-1918 veterans, many only in the 40-45 age group, very enthusiastic and professional. The Commanding

Officer (Captain Barton) was very keen and looked very fierce; he had been wounded by shrapnel in the First World War, which had caused his tin helmet to cut his face badly. It had left him with a fearsome looking scar and a dislike for tin hats, but he was a very capable officer. The few young men awaiting call-up had the best of it when it came to strenuous military exercises, crawling through the fields or crouching behind suburban garden walls. We found, however, that we "volunteered" for the unarmed combat courses and physical training courses run by Headquarters, and I was allowed to have the only Browning machine gun issued to the unit. The fact that it was heavier than the rifles issued to everybody else, only proves how professional the veterans were! The courses were run at Wembley Stadium and consisted of training by regular soldiers. There was an emphasis on physical fitness and being thrown about, as we struggled to master the art of 'silent killing' and skulduggery. One young trainee, who was paired off with me for these activities, was a professional boxer, who showed me his rippling torso, and asked me to punch him as hard as I could in his stomach. I politely declined, not that I thought he might suffer, but because I did not want to damage my knuckles or wrist! I do not think that I could have hurt him if I had jumped on his stomach with my Home Guard boots on.

Apart from regular drills and guard duties, we had mock battles with adjoining units; one unit was very put out when we sneaked in and cut their telephone wire. Not cricket, but we gave wonderful entertainment to the residents of Pinner, climbing all over their gardens, lying in the gutter and firing off crackers as simulated rifle fire. By the end of 1941 we were better equipped and trained - a real force to be reckoned with and I was proud to be part of the Middlesex "Die Hards".

My call-up papers for the R.A.F. had arrived in November 1941 but normally there was a further delay of 6 months on reporting for aircrew training, for which I had volunteered. I had to attend a Selection Board and was delighted to be accepted for immediate service without the 6 months wait, I do not think my Mother was at all pleased; my colleagues at the office who were patiently waiting, were livid!

Lord's Cricket Ground

On the 23rd of February 1942 I was ordered to report early to Air Crew Receiving Centre (A.C.R.C.) at Lords cricket ground, and as an air-crew cadet I trod the boards of the Long Room along with 2000 men on the same intake. Unfortunately for me, my immediate call up meant that my Service Number (1802854) was much greater than most of those reporting (around 1,400,000). In the Forces everything is done by numbers so I had to wait all day before I was eventually marched away with the 35th group of men. called "flights" - last of the day.

No 35 Flight - mixed bag of old sweats and new recruits at Air Crew Receiving Centre, Lords Cricket Ground (ACRC) I am 4th from left - front rank

We fed at the Zoo, very appropriate, long crocodiles of airmen marching in their flights with a red hurricane lamp swinging at the back in the pitch black winter morning. We stood in lines for everything, food, uniforms, medicals, and the dreaded inoculations. The queue for these jabs was so long that it stretched outside the building and several yards down the street This gave the humorists the chance to write on adjacent walls "three hours from here" (and it was) "abandon hope all ye who enter here" (several did and fainted) and "they've only got one needle" (and it felt like it). Our flight being the last of the intake was last in the queue for everything, including pay parade. During our course we had an inspection by the Air Officer Commanding. In theory we were stood to attention with full pack whilst he started at the first flight and finished at ours. The first flights were so far away down the road that we had the opportunity to sag quietly against the fences and gates of the houses behind us, until the A. O. C and retinue of Officers got closer - a matter of 3 hours. I suppose, on reflection, it was a marathon for them too.

We were drilled daily and marched around the Regents Park area and our corporal in charge was very popular, especially when we "fell out" by a cafe for a "cup of char and a wad" He had a tricky job for our flight of immediate entrants also contained some re-mustered ground personnel, sergeant fitters and armourers who had aspirations to fly. They out-ranked the corporal not only in rank but years of service, yet they had to toe the line as air crew cadets One advantage for the rest of us was that the tea breaks were longer and more frequent than average. The well-worn uniforms of the old hands contrasted sharply with our new issue, only the white flash in the forage caps, denoting that we were aircrew, indicated that they were under training. When they heard my service number they fell about laughing, and I heard, for the first of many times, "Get some in". My service in the Home Guard with the old sweats came in useful, not only the drill and discipline, but also the looking after Number 1. Our kit was left, laid out for inspection during the day and when I found my new pair of plimsolls - part of our new issue - had been substituted for a very old dilapidated pair, I knew where to look. Sure enough, among all the worn equipment of one of the Sergeants was a brand new pair of plimsolls, my size. He was unlucky, because although they were N.C.O's, they had to share the same billets as us, so I had the opportunity of quietly swapping the plimsolls back again. Not a word was said.

The billets were the flats along the road bordering Regents Park, Prince Albert Road, overlooking the Grand Union Canal they are still there to this day and very expensive they are, but better furnished, no doubt, than in 1942. They were stripped bare, apart from iron bedsteads, and rang to the echo of new boots and shouts of "Get fell in" on parade. The canal has not changed either, except that in those days a Sergeant or Corporal in charge of the very large flights would get too zealous and be thrown into the canal.

The more intelligent N.C.O.s in charge, realising we were only at A.C.R.C. for 3 weeks adopted a friendly manner behind the shouting and ordering about and many got a substantial sum from a whip round at the end of the course. I was able to get home to Pinner several times during the three weeks. Most of the others, who came from all over, went to the local pubs or the bright lights of the West End. The pay did not encourage many such visits, but to hear some of the boasting, the ladies of Piccadilly were believers in free love!

Newquay

The next posting changed all that, however, for the object of the Initial Training Wings (I.T.W.) was to give the new recruits a basic knowledge of Airmanship and Service Drill and, most important, get them fit. For this reason I.T.W.s were situated in seaside resorts and my posting was to Newquay, taken there direct by rail from London. The first intimation that fitness was top priority came directly we left the station for as we marched out of the forecourt carrying our kit bags, we were ordered to "double march" - running to the uninitiated. To make matters worse the road led uphill and we were soon out of breath, gasping for air and very relieved to get to our destination.

Ellis, Bower and Jennings on Tolcarne Beach, Newquay

Tolcarne Beach - Newquay 1942 - Boarding House billets located on Front

11

This was a large boarding house perched high on the cliffs overlooking Tolcarne Bay, a very healthy spot for a holiday and relaxing in the sun. The sun shone, but relax we did not; the time of the year was right, between March and June, the food, however, was very basic but adequate. The tea was allegedly laced with bromide to keep us passive and the intensive training programme kept us fully occupied, the holiday atmosphere was there somewhere; we just didn't have time to join in. We did, however get some swimming in Tolcarne Bay and with the aid of some planks of wood, simulated the surfers who ride the waves today.

The competitive spirit was encouraged between the four flights in the town, each flight about fifty men, especially in a cross-country run in which everybody participated at the end of the course. This covered physical training, small arms drill and "square bashing" on the parade ground, indoor training in classrooms on rudiments of airmanship, theory of flight, instruments, navigation and meteorology. We studied telegraphy and learnt the Morse code both on the sending key and the Aldis lamp. With the latter we retired into the hills behind Newquay and flashed messages from there to the attic room of our boarding house on the front. These messages, apart from the mistakes, never got above the "cat sat on the mat" variety, and took a long time to send and receive; all that rapid flashing seen in war films was left to the Navy.

No 1 Flight, 'A' Squadron No 7 ITW, March 1942
Back Row: Horsman, Graham, Wilcock, Patterson, Artha, Trout, Porter, Helaing, Hance, Withers
Centre 1: Brantingham, Lucas, Glansford, Bodman, Leggo, Alderton, French, Goodman, Woodhouse, Garside, Donkin, Jennings and Brear
Centre 2: Dowd, Ellis, Roberts (472), Sutherland, Wellstead, Craig, MacMillan, Northrop, Roberts (143) Long, Knight, Sarjeant, Matthews, Ford
Front Row: Purslow, Charles, Ansell, Warburton, Cox, Lupton, Riches, Nash, Taylor, Radford, Bower

The most boring duty was being on guard,(a curfew was in force for the R.A.F of 10 P.M.) so one could cheer on the late returning unfortunates at that hour. After that, one stood about armed with a pick-axe handle right through the small hours - 4 hours on, 4 hours off. For arms drill, however, we had the .303 Lee Enfield Rifle, ex 1914/1918 war, and for firing on the ranges we had the rifles and the Vickers gas operated machine gun. We did our weapons training in the lock up garages behind the boarding house, learning how to strip and clean the guns under the tuition of a sergeant who went by the book. By this, I mean he knew his guns word by word as written in the manual, it was an education to hear him describe the action of the Vickers machine gun, the phrase "rotating on its trunnions" has stuck with me all my life.

Our Physical Training Instructor (P.T.I.) was a fanatic for the compulsory inter flight cross-country and at the start of the course he assured us that we as a flight would win it. To achieve this he had us run the course two or three times a week in plimsolls to start with, but finally running in boots (issued for marching and stamping with!) On resuming plimsolls for the actual race we all flew round. I finished 4th and the three in front of me were all from our flight. Needless, to say, we won the overall race and were very fit indeed, perhaps the bromide was necessary after all!

During the six week course they broke it to us gently, that although we had all been accepted for Pilot training we were part of the Pilot = Navigator Bomb-aimer (P.N.B.) Scheme This scheme had been brought in to get crews for the heavy four-engine bombers which were being produced in ever increasing numbers, and meant that only a small proportion of those accepted for training would finish, up as pilots. The rest would be allocated to other categories of aircrew. The allocation would be made after all of us had done a minimum of 12 hours flying training in Tiger Moths, assessed on our abilities, and posted accordingly. The gentle part of telling us all this was done by an Officer, himself an Observer, who pointed out that only about 10% of us were needed for pilots and promotion would come quicker for the other categories, witness himself. Naturally we all thought we would be one of the 10% - only Spitfires or Hurricanes for us!

Ready for the open cockpit of a Tiger Moth

Ansty followed by Manchester

After a week's leave at the end of I.T.W. training at Newquay I was posted to Elementary Flying Training School (E.F.T.S.) at Ansty, near Coventry, for the 12 hours flying training. The De Haviland Tiger Moth two-seater bi-planes used for this training were a credit to the manufacturer and the fitters who serviced them, for they were subjected to violent manoeuvres and heavy landings from morn till night. The Flying Instructors, Officers and Sergeant Pilots were - 'resting', after operational tours and were hard put to it to cope with the flow of raw recruits that must have seemed like a never ending flood.

They flew all day; as they landed they took another fresh pupil, flew for about 30 minutes, did their piece, landed and took another pupil. Flying hours were chalked up in the office and whilst one pupil was in the air the rest sat around awaiting the call to fly. The standard of the instructors varied considerably and the way the training was implemented meant that one had a different instructor nearly every trip. Some were very good, calm and sensible, but others were in a state of nerves following their tour of ops, or disillusioned with having to do this training, bored with the job, when they wanted to be on an operational squadron.

One would concentrate on take-off and landings, another would be more concerned with the "Hun in the sun" and require the pupil to screw his neck rapidly from side to side looking back over his shoulder. Yet another, one of the bored type, would show his prowess at the controls, to the detriment of the pupil's stomach!

Despite these hazards, or because of them, one had to sort out the best advice and learn to fly the Tiger during the short time available - about 14 days, and although they did not realise it, the Instructors were held in some awe by their pupils, were they not of the Few? Probably not, by this time, as it was June 1942 but some of them had obviously been through frightening experiences.

Each pupil was given his total of 12 flying hours tuition and despite an attack of Montezuma's revenge (the food was awful) I completed the course and could cope with take off, landing, spinning, and not get lost too often. I should have reported sick and no doubt there were others of my colleagues on the course who were suffering, but nobody went sick, they might get left behind, or worse still be removed from a flying course altogether.

From Ansty we were posted to the collection centre at Heaton Park Manchester where all the trainees were allocated to further training under the Empire Air Training Scheme. Re-mustering, as it was called, involved going overseas to Canada, South Africa or America to complete a lengthy course in whatever trade one was allocated to. There were 7000 men waiting at Heaton Park for convoys to be organised; only a few of these were allocated to further pilot training, the rest to aircrew categories, in my case Air Bomber.

This was a new category, a division of. the existing Observers job into two separate trades. The Navigator concentrated on the charts and position of the aircraft and kept the plot i.e. did the actual navigation, the Air Bomber did the bomb aiming and release, visual map reading to aid the Navigator and act as Pilot in an emergency. The job developed later on, with the increased use of Radar, to act as Radar Operator and Front Gunner.

Manchester in summer was as one would expect - very wet! 1942 was no exception. It rained every day and we had to parade in the park every day, protected from the rain by the issued rubber cape, which doubled as a ground sheet and directed the rain directly on to one's trousers. Our billets were around the park in the suburbs of Manchester, the "landladies" supplying bed and breakfast only, after which they didn't want us around. A good billet depended on whether the landlady was trying to make a profit from the allowance for her enforced lodgers or, as sometimes happened they had their own sons in the Forces and tried to make their airmen at home. I wasn't too lucky and can remember my 20th birthday, being lined up across the top of Heaton Park in torrential rain and then proceeding forward across the park picking up any litter, including matchsticks, we could find.

For entertainment we visited the pubs, cafes and cinemas of Manchester, at least we were out of the rain some of the time. On one occasion three of us were in a bar, drowning our sorrows and one Romeo among us was talking to a very young and pretty girl. Naturally we asked whether she had any friends. 'Oh yes' she said, 'here they come now.' We were embarrassed to see, that the two 'girls' were the most made-up old tarts one could wish to meet (or rather not meet). We bought a round of drinks and suggested a visit to the cinema , anything to keep them in the dark, where they would not be seen with us! One of them commented 'why bother' but seeing our reluctance to go straight off with them, they all came to the cinema, including Romeo and the 'bait'. There was a long queue outside, which we joined, so leaving Romeo to his fate I took the other airman by the arm, suggesting that he and I would check at the Box Office. We went into the foyer and I explained the situation to the usherette on the door. I suspect that she had heard it all before, because she smiled and took us straight through the middle of the cinema and let us out of the back door!. We made our way back to camp, and when Romeo returned later he told us that after waiting some time, they went off looking for some other punters. We did not uphold the gentlemanly tradition of the R.A.F. but we had at least taken in the warning horror films about prostitutes!.

Hastings

There was a delay in getting the overseas posting organised so we Air Bombers to be were sent to Hastings, our destination the Marine Court, on the front at St. Leonards.on.Sea. This block of flats resembles an ocean liner with the curved appearance at one end, the "bridge", which was part of the Marine Court Hotel. Most of the other Hotels and Boarding Houses on the sea front had been requisitioned for the forces, which was also true of most of the holiday towns in the Country. Our new luxury accommodation was stripped bare, like those at St. John's Wood, at least four men to a room, but we did have a bathroom adjacent - no plugs in the sink or bath naturally, a peculiarity of life in the Service. We won the approval of the Flight Sergeant in charge by buying some cleaner between us and polishing up the bath, removing several layers of scum. The food was very good. The R.A.F. did the catering, and the hotel ballroom was large enough for all of us for meals, and we soon made ourselves at home.

Marine Court, St Leonards on Sea, still there today

18

The Beach & Grand Parade, St. Leonards-on-Sea. 15447

Regular route marches, parades, physical training, football matches and classroom training kept us fit and occupied. One day in September, however, we were returning in three separate flights from a route march. We were stretched out on a hill going down behind the Marine Court flats when with a snarl and a roar a Focke Wulf 190, one of a pair, appeared over the flats in front of us. It was climbing up, a full plan view, easily recognisable, especially the bomb which it had just released and was heading straight for us. There was only one thing we could do and that was flatten on the road and pray. I finished up in the gutter with only the kerb for protection. The aircraft had aimed the bomb at the flats but left its release too late, so it fell on the road behind the flats and by a lucky chance for the F.W.190 we were there. It landed with an ear-splitting crunch on a house alongside our flight and enveloped us with brick dust and chunks of debris. Through this cloud, as we struggled to sort ourselves out, came shouts of "down, down" for the F.W. had been joined by it's partner and was attacking us and the other flights further up the hill with cannon and machine guns.

The sole opposition they had from us, was one solitary Vickers machine gun mounted on the roof of the flats, manned by whoever was on the duty rota. The airman on duty this particular day was a brave man for he let fly several magazines at the F.W.s without any noticeable effect; he was very exposed on the flat roof. They in turn were firing at us on the

19

road and he was well within their sights - we were more of a target no doubt. There were some Bofors guns in the town manned by Canadian soldiers, but they were too far away to help much. Eventually the two aircraft flew off, one trailing smoke or fuel and we limped back to the flats for a roll call and check on casualties.

Luckily these were light, the bomb had demolished an unoccupied house which had taken the full force of the explosion and although several men were injured with fragments of cannon shells, and others had bad bruises from flying bricks, there were no fatalities that I knew of.

I had a bruise in the ribs from a brick and a cut knee from diving in the gutter, my uniform was a delicate pink from brick dust. After a clean up I reported for the roll call, only to be told that I should have reported first; they had me down as a casualty . The second F.W. had been more successful in aiming it's bomb, in that it had lobbed into the flats, raising a cheer from a. flight marching along the sea front. The bomb caused minor damage to the building, which was deserted due to all flights being out marching about. The raid was part of a series by the Luftwaffe, hit and run tactics, on the obvious targets, troops in hotels on the seafront all along the coast.

No doubt their reconnaissance aircraft had filmed the marching activities of the blue clad airmen to and from the Marine Court, it was a wonderful target, and the attack certainly had an effect. That same night following the bombing, we were raised from our beds, ordered to pack and as dawn broke we were marching again, this time in single file down the road to the railway station. We carried our own kit bags on our shoulders and overhead were a patrol of Typhoon fighters, the R.A.F.'s. ' answer in speed to the F.W. 190, someone was taking no chances!

Harrogate-Blackpool-Liverpool

We left the 'Battle of Hastings 1942. from the railway station at St. Leonards-on-Sea and embarked on a very long train journey. It was the first time that I realised that it was, and is, possible to cross London by rail without changing at one of the main stations. After passing London we continued North and it became very much colder at our destination - Harrogate. We were temporarily billeted in a girls school on the outskirts of the town in Pannal Ash, probably the same school with the bell marked "ring for mistress". I cannot remember whether the bells rang all night but I know that our stay was brief, for we were soon moved on to Blackpool, home of the famous landladies.

They were well used to transient airmen, for their boarding houses were the last billets before overseas postings. We were kitted out with tropical khaki shirts, shorts and socks, a fair indication that we were going somewhere warmer than Blackpool in October. The rumour mongers had us all over the world, the tropical kit was just a ruse, a deception to foil the Germans, when we boarded a ship it would all be changed for heavy winter clothing, so they said.

We would have welcomed that, for we embarked at Liverpool on H.M.T.B.5. (better known as the Stirling Castle) on a very cold day and lay at anchor opposite the Royal Liver Building for what seemed an eternity. It was a week at least, just waiting, not allowed on shore, our letters written with the code address H.M.T.B.5., but what could one say - the censor would not let anything vital get through, and the mail would not be posted until we were long departed.

One morning, however, we rolled out of our hammocks to find that we had sailed overnight, and the deck under our feet had a peculiar movement to it. When we were allowed up from our mess-deck we could see that we had been joined by a convoy of several large troopships and, more comforting, a large section of the Royal Navy.

Conditions on the Sterling Castle varied according to the rank and status of the individual. The accommodation available was divided

21

roughly into three parts, the first part occupied by 150 Wrens, the second by 500 officers, and the third by 5000 men. The upper decks with cabins and room to move about were used by the officers and the Wrens and fraternisation was allowed. Not so for the licentious soldiery; the 5000 men were contingents of R.A.F. airmen going to South Africa for training and Army units going to India and Burma via the Cape, their quarters were below decks and there they were to remain. Everybody did get together for boat drill however, it was necessary for us to attend regular drills on the upper decks, gazing out at other ships in the convoy, and watching the horizon going up and down as the ship rolled. Gazing up at the Officers and Wrens fraternising on the top decks seemed to affect a number of the men - they had a wistful look about them.

It was as well that the weather was so awful and the sea so rough, nobody stayed up on deck long except for those poor unfortunates that were sea sick permanently. They stood as far as they could from the rail only dashing over at the last minute, lashed by the wind and the rain I think some of them would have liked to jump over the side.

The mess deck, that we occupied, was fitted out with long tables and benches screwed to the floor. Above were slung the hammocks, which took some time to master the art of getting in and out, without going into a nose dive. One member in turn from each table went off to the galley to collect the food for the rest of the men at his table. Meals were very good to start with, but deteriorated in quality as time went on, especially the eggs which got so bad that one time when they arrived in a bucket at the end of the table, they were passed rapidly the complete length of the table and jettisoned through the porthole in one swift movement, Heaven help any U boat that picked up that lot!

One could purchase chocolate and sweets from the ship's shop for a while, but supplies soon ran out. The weather was too rough for food to be too important and October in the Atlantic was not the time for cruising. Most of us soon got our 'sea legs' and then food did become important; the threat from dive-bombers and U-boats was left to the Royal Navy. They soon left us to our own devices, however, which consisted of zigzagging endlessly, just three liners (Stirling Castle, Monarch of Bermuda, and an Empress class vessel)tossing about like toy boats but moving slowly south, which at least meant an improvement in the weather. (We were not told that the escort had been diverted to cover the 'Torch' North African convoys.)

As we entered the tropics life below decks became torrid, not improved at night with a 'blacking out' of all the light and most of the chances of a breath of air. Many of us forsook the hammocks swinging in the hot air above the tables, for the hopefully cooler mess deck floor under the tables We just lay on a blanket on the floor and slept as best we could, perspiration rolled off us, all things considered there was no chance of us getting fat

To keep us occupied, apart from the boat drills and odd lectures, we had a pep talk from the Wing Commander Paul Richey, on his way to India in charge of the RAF contingent. He was an ex Battle of Britain pilot, rows of medals and obviously some sort of god to all of us The subject of his talk, inspired by Air Ministry no doubt, was how great it was to be a member of the Air Force, and that we were Ambassadors abroad, all of which we knew, but would have preferred a blow by blow account of his fighter activities We had plenty of spare time and there were all sorts of card schools, pound notes flashed at 'Crown and Anchor. but this activity was confined mainly to the Army and Merchant Seamen aboard; not much gambling for the RAF cadets, their pay wasn't up to it. A friend and I played chess with a pocket set which was useful as the pieces fitted into slots and the rolling of the ship did not stop us playing. We used to find a sunny spot on deck, and played innumerable games, we were about the same standard so that neither gained too big a lead of wins. Such concentrated chess improved our standard and we entered a chess tournament organised by some real experts, not expecting to get beyond the first round. I was beaten in the final, mainly due to surprise and nerves at having got so far!

We were at sea a whole month before we reached our first port of call, not our final destination; to our amazement we sailed into the port of Bahia in South America, where we took on water and fresh vegetables. The Wing Commander's talk on ambassadors made sense, for we were paraded and marched around the town, through the crowds who stood and applauded, cheering and waving as if we were RAF veterans already. It was very colourful after the weeks at sea, but apart from a march round we were not allowed ashore. Somebody slipped up, for after we set sail again rumour had it that several soldiers had taken the opportunity to disappear during the march. They were aware that they were due for the real war in India and Burma and preferred to take a chance in South America. There may be Nazis in Argentina but I wonder if there are some of our ex-soldiers still in Brazil? (Friends of Ronnie Biggs, no doubt).

The final ten days of our voyage took us into stormy weather again, I stood at the stern of the Stirling Castle which was a fairly large ship about 20000 tons, watching the huge waves rearing up behind us, and tossing us aside; the other two liners disappearing in the troughs and rolling as we were, one felt very insignificant indeed - storms at sea are not for the faint-hearted.

South Africa

Six weeks after leaving Liverpool we arrived at Durban complete with the 'lady in white' as she was known, (Perla Gibson) singing patriotic songs to us, through a megaphone, as we sailed into the harbour. We lined the rails, which caused a list to starboard, cheering like mad and waving to the people on shore, we were late for the relief of Mafeking, but we were there in South Africa at last! We had no opportunity to see Durban, straight on to a train and off journeying again. We realised it was no short trip when we were issued with blankets and allocated to bunks; we exchanged the rocking motion of the boat for that of the train. (The journey now is called the Eastern Cape and Garden Route' a popular holiday trip)

When night fell, the noise from the country-side was terrific; whirring and chirping from all sides, but at least there was no black-out, and one could see the carriage lights reflected on the passing country; a strange sight after 3 years of drawn blinds and curtains. By daylight we were passing through mountainous scenery, very different from the lush green of England. The country-side was heat scorched, but beautiful in its own way. The railway wound through the hills and around, taking all one day to travel from the top of one mountain to the floor of the valley, and eventually puffed into the small coastal town of East London.

Our training as Air Bombers started at 48 Air School, just outside the town. The camp was perched up on the cliffs overlooking the sea, and the climate was wonderful for it was their Summer. The mornings, or at least the early morning at 6.30a.m. when we were roused, were very cold but the sun soon warmed things up. Ablutions in cold water at 6.30 under a corrugated roof, with no other shelter, was Spartan, a typical attitude of the South Africans, some of whom were in training with us. Facilities were very basic, toilets had no doors, and a favourite sport was to climb up inside the next toilet to the one occupied, lean over the top and pull the chain. The seated occupant got a cold shower and a set of brass monkeys! When the sun rose it got very warm indeed and we were glad of the khaki

(Above) Horseman, Hance, Jennings, Goodman, Lawley - At 48 Air School East London, S Africa

(Left) Jennings/Hance (My chess opponent on the Stirling Castle - he was killed on a training flight at 16 Operational Training Unit Upper Heyford, Oxford in 1943

uniforms, although we dispensed with the issued Boer War type pith helmets and wore forage caps.

The local people in East London were very hospitable and invited us into their homes, the restaurants and cafes were an eye-opener to our home rationed style of living. Steaks, butter and eggs, all in profusion plus exotic forms of fruit and vegetables, many of which we had never seen before, like paw-paws and passion fruits.

I spent Christmas Day 1942 with some South African friends on the beach; we had lunch in a restaurant adjacent to the shore, typical Christmas fare - yes, turkey and the trimmings followed by pudding soaked in Brandy! Temperatures were in the 80's and we were pleased to follow the meal with a nap stretched out on the sand under beach umbrellas. Later, we swam in the surf, which made our waves at Newquay look like a millpond, and finished off the afternoon with large helpings of ice cream. Christmas has never been the same since!

The flying training took place at another Air School, No. 44 at Grahamstown, inland from East London, navigation training in Ansons and Bombing training in Oxfords, both small twin-engine planes. The pilots were South African, some experienced from the fighting in the Middle East, and others newly trained. I found one of the latter the hard way, for on our first flight in an Anson listed as "air experience" the pilot could not find out how to get the wheels up after take off. After several circuits he decided to land again and find out. Long after everybody else had disappeared over the horizon he taxied in and called over a mechanic. The simple answer was a jack handle inserted under the front seat which wound the undercarriage up or let it down. The inexperience showed on both sides, for it fell to us occupying the second pilot's seat to do the physical job of winding it up or down - about 147 turns up and 100 down (it came down faster under it's own weight). We knew all about it by the time we had flown many trips, 147 turns up was monotonous, not to say tiring!

Further flights in the Anson were for map reading and passing pin points (exact position on the map in longitude and latitude) to the embryo Navigators, who, like us, were very green, not only as beginners but often in the face due to the hot bumpy weather! Toilets on the Ansons did not exist; sole means of relieving oneself was a funnel that was attached to a tube leading to the outside of the aircraft. This funnel was anchored to the fuselage near the rear door and worked well, unless some poor soul had tried to be sick into it, causing a blockage, with dire results all round.

Amidst all the turbulence the Navigators struggled with their charts and logs trying to keep to their flight plan, they had little time to look outside and see where they were. The country- side was mostly scrub with mountains on one side and a few rivers leading down to the sea on the other, towns were few, so that at night one could see the lights many miles away. Most of the routes we flew were from town to town and back to base, so that one could see where we should be heading, and many a wrong course, given by the Navigator to the Pilot, was ignored, because we would have been heading hopelessly out to sea

We flew most days, for the weather was perfect, there were thunderstorms and occasional fogs but they cleared quickly. I was surprised at first in Grahamstown by the size of the gutters in the streets, they were very wide and deep, but when the first storm came I saw the reason. The storms were tropical, beautiful violet lightning with the rain like a waterfall, soon filling the gutters which became small rivers, The water rapidly dried up when the storm blew over, and although these were intense they did not last long. The fog was rare, but accounted for our first casualty; a Crew in an Oxford returning from practice bombing was caught low in fuel, with fog over the 'drome, so the pilot and two trainee Air Bombers had to bale out. One of the latter landed heavily and broke an ankle, but carried on with the course; plastered foot and a stick wasn't going to hold him back! The only other casualty we had during this course was a cadet underneath an Oxford on the ground checking the loading of the practice- smoke bombs. His colleague inside the aircraft accidentally released one, which fell alongside him on the ground, exploding and spraying his leg with the chemical contents that normally caused the smoke. This liquid burnt him badly, the skin on his leg looked like cardboard, but he too; carried on with the course, despite a severe limp.

The bombing ranges were not far from our airfield at Grahamstown so that we were able to carry out several flights a day. The targets, in the form of wooden triangles, were set out in the bush, with two observation towers at a respectable distance to plot the fall of the smoke bombs, and report, back to our base. Each tower would give a direction and distance of the exploding bomb, where the two lines crossed was plotted on a chart: so that when we returned to base our results were waiting to be assessed.

At night we used flash bombs instead of smoke; these were easier to see when dropped astray, one could look all over the place for a smoke bomb that had missed the target by thousands of yards, the flash was a sure give-away. Being set in open country the target triangle was easy to see, but the primitive bombsight and method of controlling the approach to the target made for some errors. There were no houses or people near the ranges, but we did hear of the odd claim for a cow "damaged" by our efforts.

The bombsight we used had not developed much since the First World War and relied on a hand held computer to get and set the right bombing angles. From our position in the nose of the Oxford, prone on the floor, we gave instructions to the pilot by raising a left or right leg to indicate which way we wanted him to steer to get the target in our sights. The pilots were very adept at banking round in tight circles over the target and skilled at small heading adjustments as we waggled our legs. The secret of accurate bombing was for the aircraft to be flying level at a steady speed and height when the bomb was released. Too often the aircraft was halfway through a course correction, or coming out of a split-arse turn, so that the bomb was thrown off into the wilds. Nevertheless, by peering out of the aircraft itself, seeing where the bomb landed and getting the plots from the observation towers, not too many got away.

We improved; our leg work from the floor of the aircraft became more sophisticated; a small shake meant a small correction, a frantic wave meant we were miles off, the pilots got to flying straight and level, so that results became respectable.

In addition to high level bombing from 10,000ft, we practised low level bombing and gunnery, both air to sea firing and ,air to air. A very brave pilot flew a Fairy Fulmer fighter towing a drogue, whilst we shot at it, the drogue that is, not the Fulmer! Although the patches on the tail of the Fulmer could tell another story. My air to air efforts in shooting at the drogue (a long sausage looking target) ended abruptly when a lucky (?) shot severed the towing wire and the drogue sailed off on ifs own, to drift down into the sea.

The road from Port Elizabeth to Grahamstown March 1943

View from the top of a lorry - the donkeys were often faster than the lorry!

Ostrich in the wild

The gunnery training was carried out at Port Elizabeth on the coast some miles from Grahamstown; firing of guns in the air was safer over the sea for all concerned. To get to the airfield at Port Elizabeth we were loaded on to lorries and it took about 2.1/2hours through the bush and scrub to get there. The dust raised by these lorries penetrated everywhere, so, despite the heat we wore our flying kit which zipped up to the neck like overalls. To avoid the shaking and battering from the lorries on the rough tracks, we climbed up on to the canvas roof and rode on top, hanging on for dear life. We did not enjoy the journey, but were kept amused by the ostrich racing about the bush , running faster than the truck, also they often stood and gazed at us - poor fools, perched on top of a lorry

Night bombing resumed after that., back at Grahamstown,

We often made two trips in a night, dropping eight flash bombs on each trip to the ranges. With the night flying and the lack of sleep we became exhausted, so that when we eventually staggered off to our hut in the early dawn we fell. log like, into our beds. Of course, life on the camp went on as usual and nobody bothered to tell the Orderly Officer or inspecting Sergeant that we had been flying all night. To give this official pair credit, when they flung open the door on one occasion and shouted "stand by your beds" all they got was a series of groans and mutters about pushing off. Instead of rousting everybody out they quietly closed the door and crept away. They came back later, however, discipline was maintained, for the Air School was run by the South African Air Force, organised along Army lines. Their uniforms and rank were those of the Army, the pilots were all Lieutenants and the drill Sergeants were army trained, no touch of the Brylcream boys with them.

We had been marching and drilling and mounting guard on two very old aircraft, not to mention the rest of the camp, all through our course, When this came to an end the drill Sergeants took us over. They had to lick us into shape for the "passing-out" parade at which we were presented with our aircrew "air bomber" berets, the half wing with a 'B' in the middle.

A very impressive occasion for us, a march past the Base Commander with all units on the base taking part, including a band plus goat as mascot to lead us. We had finished our overseas training.

Wings Parade

Line up after Wings Parade April 1943

End of course 'Wings Dinner The 3073 was a form on which the bombs were plotted by the embryo Air Bombers. Comments about each member were by mutual consensus and heavily censored

We had a final 'Wings Dinner' in Grahamstown, at which several compliments were paid to us by the instructors in their speeches. The final speech was to be given by our Course Leader, one Corporal Fred Mustoe, whose sole word of command was 'Rightho', several brandies seemed to have robbed him of his voice, so another cadet had to make an impromptu speech, which mercifully was quite short.

Menu

o:o:o

Consomme a la Royale

o:o:o

Fried Silver Bream Au Citroen

o:o:o

Asparagus en Branches Butter Sauce

o:o:o

Crumbed Lamb Cutlets Petit Pois

o:o:o

Roast Stuffed Chicken and French Salad
Roast Sirloin Beef and Horseradish Sauce
Roast Lamb and Mint Sauce

o:o:o

Baked Potatoes   Boiled Potatoes
Green Peas   Cabbage

o:o:o

Wine Trifle
Vanilla Ice Cream

o:o:o

Coffee

Return Home

There followed some quick interviews, the first with the Course and Base Commanders, the essence of which was that they needed us - the British - in their Country, please come back to South Africa after the war. How right they were, but how many went back? A few of us were selected for promotion to commissioned rank and offered the opportunity to stay on as Instructors. Our enthusiasm for getting home was such that we all declined the offer; with hindsight, we would have seen the war out comfortably. Many did just that in South Africa and Rhodesia, but call it what you will - homesickness, patriotism, pride or just getting on with the job - we all opted to return.

Events moved fast, we were sent by train to Cape Town, where within two days, we newly commissioned Officers were shipped aboard T.M.S. Dempo, a 17,000 ton Dutch Liner en route to England. This was a complete contrast to our journey out - no convoy - one ship on a fast run home - no stops, steaming as quickly as it could with no zigs and no zags. Apart from the crew and ourselves, there were no other Service passengers, some civilians were on priority passage and associated with government departments. One group was an E.N.S.A. concert party returning to England but we never had the opportunity to see their show. The best entertainment turned out to be the job given to the R.A.F. contingent - we were all requisitioned to man the Bofors anti-aircraft guns!

We became part of the crew, and after a crash course on how to aim and fire the guns, we stood the same watches as the crew, but took our meals in the dining room along with the other passengers. This proved tricky, for they ate at logical times and we were in and out like rabbits, as our turn came for duty. The Head Waiter looked after us very well and would always produce a meal, whatever the hour.

We must have been a source of comfort to the civilians, these keen eyed R.A.F. boys manning the guns, the rest of the crew probably thought otherwise. Whilst on duty at gun positions, we were linked to each other and the Bridge by telephone and kept watch for any unusual movements by day, or strange lights at night on the surrounding waters. There were several movements on deck at night among the civilians, male and female, which were duly reported between gun positions and comments on the charms of the female passengers sun bathing on deck during the day; we certainly kept a sharp look out all round. We had only two heart stopping moments whilst I was on watch; the first a report from 'A' gun position, that there was a light on the horizon. This was confirmed in broken English from the Bridge as "yee moon eez rizing". The second, in daylight, an aircraft flew rapidly towards us, so we manned the guns expecting trouble, but it proved to be one of ours on reconnaissance.

Our accommodation was an improvement on the Stirling Castle, four of us shared a cabin, but as we were on different watches we were never all in the cabin at the same time. The voyage out to South Africa via South America had taken us 6 weeks, the return voyage direct took only 17 days to Liverpool from the Cape. The Dempo (subsequently sunk in landings around Italy) slowed down only on the last morning as we crept through a mist, with the sea so smooth that the only ripples were caused by the ship, to drop anchor back on the Mersey.

We returned immediately from the ship to Harrogate to await a further

posting, and get kitted out as Officers. We had not had time to get new uniforms in South Africa before embarking and had managed in battledress (standard issue tunic and trousers worn by all ranks in wartime) on the ship. We discovered one major difference from our previous visit to Harrogate. Then we had only held the dizzy rank of Leading Aircraftmen and were shouted at - now we were requested politely by a Warrant Officer to "get fell in gentlemen!", I can imagine his feelings towards these obviously "sprog" (green) Officers in their new uniforms!

Doug Jennings back from South Africa

Staverton-Manby

In order to accustom us to flying conditions in England our next posting was to an Advanced Flying Unit (A.F.U.) at Staverton in Gloucestershire, where we flew night and day bombing and navigation trips once again in Anson aircraft. Night trips were vastly different from those in South Africa; the bright lights of the towns were replaced by flashing beacons denoting the positions of aerodromes; they had a habit of disappearing suddenly if enemy aircraft were around. Bombing targets included infrared lights on the ground which were invisible from the aircraft, but left a trace on film. One would be given just the map reference and position, (e.g. near Wallingford, Oxon) and aim at a spot in the dark. Pressing the bomb release exposed the film and when this was processed one either had a trace, or a blank. This was known as "camera bombing". The target at Wallingford was very difficult but situated on an island in the river; on a moonlit night the reflection of the Thames was a great help.

At the conclusion of this course, by now the end of July 1943, I expected to go to an Operational Training Unit for crewing up, but three of us were sent off for specialist training to No.1. Air Armament School at Manby in Lincolnshire. A new bombsight, the Mark XIV was being introduced into Bomber Command and we were to be initiated into the way it worked. The course was run by Squadron Leader Richardson, a real enthusiastic and dedicated Instructor. He was an expert on 'Bombs and Comps', as bombs and components were known, and later became Bombing Leader of 617 Squadron.

No night flying was involved, but the course was very hectic, the aircraft used were old Blenheims, a twin engine bomber in service at the beginning of the war. They were flown, with some dash, by Polish pilots - the mad Poles as we called them- they loved to fly at low level. Because we were also testing a new low level bombsight, we had the opportunity of experiencing their skill. Luckily we had plenty to do lining up the aircraft and adjusting the bombsight on the way to the target, which was located on the sands at Theddlethorpe, just off the coast from Manby.

We would take off, flash across the countryside at hedge top level (thank goodness this part of Lincolnshire was flat) and from the nose of the aircraft we appeared to dive towards the target - I'm sure we often flew in the troughs of the waves.

We learnt a great deal at Manby about all sorts of bombs and fuses and the new Mark XIV which functioned similar to the computer of today. The relevant information required for accurate bomb release (e.g. height, speed, wind direction and speed) was fed in, and the sight was stabilised by gyros so that steep turns and evasive action were allowed for. A light showed the point at which the bombs should be released on a sight glass in the form of a sword, through which one observed the target. When the hasp of the sword crossed the target was the calculated time of release. It was fascinating to see all the inventive genius and engineering that had gone into this bombsight.

It was also very sobering to see the genius that had gone into the fuses and components of the captured German bombs and mines that we took to pieces. No praise is too high for the Bomb disposal men who first fathomed out the intricate magnets, springs and booby traps on those German weapons.

At the end of this course, which took a month, I was sent on leave, and then posted to No. 16 Operational Training Unit (O.T.U.) at Upper Heyford near Oxford, to crew up and get experience of flying in heavy bombers; the aircraft used were Wellingtons.

Upper Heyford-Banbury-Scampton

The "crewing up" process was very democratic. A total complement of 15 crews, that is 15 Pilots, 15 Navigators, 15 Air Bombers, 15 Wireless Operators and 15 Rear Gunners were gathered together in one large room and told to sort themselves out into 15 complete crews. Thus one had small groups of, say, a Pilot and Navigator looking for a Wireless Operator, or an Air Bomber and a Gunner looking for a Pilot, and then having found their choice going on to another category until complete crews were assembled.

It was haphazard in one way, and no crew member really knew the capabilities or otherwise of the others, for they had never met or flown together, before this posting. It said a good deal for the thorough training of all the individual crew members that most of them went on to work well together, became firm friends and faced the future, which wasn't very bright, with an air of unconcern.

Thus I met nearly all the other members of the crew with whom I would go to War (the extra Gunner and Flight Engineer needed for the 4 engine bombers joined us later). The Pilot (a Sergeant - rank did not matter - in any case promotion was rapid for the survivors) was named Guilyn (William) Guy, a Welshman with a fair complexion and sand coloured hair immediately nicknamed 'Ginger'. The Navigator was from Bungay in Suffolk named Victor Spalding (Flying Officer) the Wireless Operator from Cleethorpes Lincs, named Grenville Hyde (Sergeant) tall and slim, nicknamed "Lofty". The Rear Gunner (another Welshman) was named Eric Raffles (Sergeant) nicknamed 'Taffy'.

The Wellington, that we were to train on, had been first class front line aircraft, and had earned a reputation for being able to take punishment. There were many tales of Wellington - or Wimpeys as they were called - staggering back from raids badly shot up. Now they were facing an even tougher hazard, 'sprog' crews, with worried pilots and even more worried instructors, dropping in like a ton of bricks during their 'circuits and bumps' (Training jargon for take off and landing practice). We had

37

Air bombers at 16 OTU (Operational Training Unit) Upper Heyford where they 'crewed up' with pilots, navigators, wireless operators and rear gunners

proof that the aircraft had been well used the day following our first flight. We were passing the hanger where the aircraft we had been flying in the day before was under routine inspection and jacked up to take the weight off the undercarriage. The Flight Sergeant in charge called us over and pointed out that the wings were showing an abnormal droop rather like a tired penguin, they were about to take the only cure available - scrap the lot!

Flying training concentrated on crew performance and took place both at Upper Heyford and its satellite airfield Barford St. John near Banbury. We spent many hours day and night, waiting to fly on long cross country trips, usually culminating in practice bombing on one of the ranges dotted about the country. We flew in all weathers, good training for operations the old hands told us, it's always bad on ops (which wasn't true) and simulated attacks on unsuspecting English towns. The searchlight batteries in these towns were given the chance to try and 'cone' us; they must have wondered why their targets didn't twist and turn like the enemy; strict limits were put on our old aircraft to keep them in one piece.

We did get one step nearer the real thing. One of our flights was part of a diversion, for we joined in a feint attack across the North Sea towards North Germany, turning back after a few hours flying. The Main

Force of bombers crossed the enemy coast to the South. Their target was Berlin, and it is to be hoped that some baffled Luftwaffe pilots waited around Hamburg for us, whilst we made our camera bombing attack on Newcastle!

Ginger Guy, our pilot, soon settled down to flying the Wellington, and as there was dual control in the aircraft he let me practice handling the controls and communicating on the R/T (Radiotelephone) with our Base; a precaution for later on, should he be injured. Vic Spalding, the Navigator, was very accurate in getting us about the involved routes, and giving me accurate information on wind speeds and directions for the bombing runs. We didn't get lost, and we managed to get our stick of bombs 45 yards from the target! Lofty Hydes, the Wireless Operator, kept in touch with Base for any special messages and produced fixed positions for Vic. These fixes were fine when flying over this country, but were jammed when it got to the operational flying over Germany. Our rear gunner "Taffy" Raffles must have been fed up with going round and round on the practice bombing runs, but enjoyed himself on the simulated attacks by a Hurricane fighter, when he used a camera gun.

At Barford St. John, the satellite airfield, we had the company of E 28/39 Prototype jet fighter with the Whittle engine. This was top secret (September 1943) and we were under close censorship not to say anything off the station, and our mail was censored. The prototype flew from the other end of the airfield and was so fast that it vanished very quickly, so we did not see much of it, in any case, we had other things to worry about.

The censor caught up with me, however, for I wrote to an Air Bomber who had been on my course in South Africa, that a mutual friend had been killed. This friend had been my chess opponent on the ship to South Africa; their aircraft had crashed on take-off, all the crew being killed. I was summoned before the Security Squadron Leader because I had mentioned the crash in the letter. This, it appeared, was vital information to the enemy. The fact that the aircraft had crashed in a field alongside the main road to Oxford, for all to see, wasn't relevant.

Oxford and Banbury were our local nightspots, the former had some good pubs and for culture one evening the whole crew went to see the ballet (Swan Lake). The ballerinas were built on the heavy side - I expect they worked in a factory all day - but they put their all into the action. We were in the front row of the Stalls, and as they landed on our side of the stage the dust rose in clouds. We, too, all rose as one man during the intervals and headed for the bar. We enjoyed the performance, which improved tremendously after the second interval.

Apart from the pubs in Banbury, one evening we found a restaurant that was serving steaks, a rare thing in wartime, although it could have been horse that we were eating (and probably was) we enjoyed the meal. With all this eating and drinking we didn't get fat, for transport was limited and we had to hike the 6 miles from Banbury to camp. The nights were often frosty and the hedge sparkled, we walked fast to keep warm, with frequent stops to inspect the hedges!

Keeping warm was a problem in our Nissen huts at Barford; the permanent station at Upper Heyford used the married quarters (a small estate of houses) Barford was a completely hutted station, all the buildings except the Watchtower were huts. We had a stove in the middle of the hut, which at times was red hot, but insulation on the corrugated iron roof was negligible. It was reminiscent of our old Anderson shelter at home, and used to run with condensation. The cold weather was a help to us in one way, one of the many crew drills we practised was dinghy drill, and with the pool frozen over we were spared the 'wet' performance. This would have meant diving, fully clothed with flying kit, into the pool and turning the inflated dinghy right way up. With this drill, and the baling out procedure each member of the crew had a specific task and order to leave the aircraft, should the necessity arise, either ditching in the sea or parachuting out. We got very adept at leaving the dummy aircraft set up in the hanger by constant practice, but with a few bruises; we were preparing for emergencies that came quickly in our war!

One night at Upper Heyford we were issued with local maps and loaded on to buses with all the windows blacked out, driven into the country for some distance and off-loaded with the instruction to find our own way back. We were not allowed to speak to anybody and we were to assume that we were in hostile country. Members of the R.A.F. police and the local police force would be searching for us, and we were to evade capture and return to Base.

By a lucky guess in finding a pinpoint on the map, I was soon on the way back, but found the going hard across very wet and muddy fields. I anticipated that the crossroads would be patrolled, so kept well clear and used minor roads heading in the right direction. Eventually I arrived on the far side of the airfield, away from the hangers and the other buildings, and was amazed to find the C.O., who had sent us out on this little jaunt, riding around on a jeep, potting at rabbits in the headlights with a 12 bore shotgun.

In wartime these headlights were hooded to a slit, to prevent any light shining up, but in the process they lost a fair amount of forward light too. The C.O. may have seen the rabbits in the light , but just beyond was me, the trainee evader, so I faded into the night and enjoyed the bacon and eggs laid on for us in the Mess. I did not realise it then, but that training was to come in useful.

Apart from my dual Instruction by Ginger Guy in flying the Wellington, I spent several hours in the 'Link' trainer, which simulated flying on instruments. When the hood of the trainer was closed down, the instructor gave directions over the headphones. He was seated at a table near the machine and the courses one flew were plotted on a chart in front of him. He would give courses, heights and speeds to fly for various patterns such as T, V, and Maltese cross, and simulated cross-country flights. We were given an assessment of ability at the end of the course that was entered in our flying logbook. I had enjoyed it and passed as "good average". Some of my friends found it claustrophobic under the hood and became disorientated, which enlivened the routine of the instructor, but left the pupil dizzy and sick.

The other test, which was also marked up in our logbooks, was for us all as a crew to be taken up to 25,000ft in a decompression chamber wearing our oxygen masks. Lofty and Vic then took their masks off and started writing a short message on a pad. In no time at all their writing became squiggly and eventually they lost consciousness, their pencils sliding aimlessly off the pad. We were very relieved to see them recover when we put their masks back on; it was a dramatic way of showing us what could happen without oxygen, made even more dramatic when they both said that at no time did they realise they were going under

We had a further period of waiting at the end of the 0.T.U. course, before our conversion to four engine aircraft, and we were posted to Scampton, an airfield just North of Lincoln. It was being converted from a grass field to concrete runways, and later became a base for 617 (dam busters) Squadron; we spent four weeks marching about in the fog and being lectured. We did get the opportunity to visit Lincoln, and the seaside at Skegness, the former dominated by the beautiful Cathedral and the town overflowing with aircrew from all the bomber bases around, causing a grave shortage of glasses. Bottles were pressed into service, the tops were sliced off and the base was used as beer glasses. Although 'shorts' were scarce; all gone for the Americans in Nottingham we were told; the beer kept flowing and the brewers were kept at full stretch; apart from the cinemas and the odd dance, entertainment was self made in the pub. One's capacity for beer grew with practice, and I suspect the strength of the drink grew weaker as the demand increased; a few more gallons of the Trent or the Witham helped the brewer's dilemma! The self entertainment may have seemed noisy to some, especially when the singing got going on such songs as "When there isn't a girl about" or the "One eyed Reilly". There was also the sense of comradeship and the determination to master "Cardinal Puff". This latter was a game where one individual had to repeat gestures by 'Cardinal Puff' in between swigging beer. If a mistake occurred, his glass was refilled and he started again. It needed a good memory and a clear head to succeed. These were the last good times that many of the participants enjoyed.

Skegness, too, was overflowing with the armed forces, but mostly naval trainees from H.M.S. Royal Arthur, otherwise known as Butlins Holiday Camp! There were RAF ground staff trainees billeted in the hotels on the front, and together with the naval ratings they caused a problem. They had all learnt the correct way. Navy or R.A.F., to salute and when Ginger, who had just been commissioned, Vic and I appeared, they were delighted to use us for saluting practice. We took to nipping off down side streets and skulking in pubs, (at least that is the reason we gave) it was in a hotel bar in fact that we nearly became involved in our own war.

A crew from Coastal Command were stood at the bar, well tanked up, and had passed from the "warm glow of friendship" in their drinking, to the "let's have a fight" stage. Our arrival at this moment brought forth the comment "bomber bastards" - not the kind of language to use to a redheaded Welshman like 'Ginger' Guy. Mayhem broke out and fists flew in all directions, the bar cleared rapidly, two of us grabbed Ginger before the furniture became involved, and exited through the swing doors.

The other crew may have been entitled to let off steam, who knows what looking for 'U' boats up to 12 or 14 hours at a time did to the nerves. We were not even operational, we needed Ginger in one piece, although his troubles were yet to come. We may have saved him from physical hurt, but a fortnight later, after we had started our conversion course at Wigsley near Lincoln. he suffered a different sort of humiliation.

Wigsley-Syerston

We were converting on to Stirlings, very large 4 engine bombers, some operational squadrons still used them, but they were used mainly for training. They had many troubles in service, with their mixed hydraulic and electrical systems, plus a complicated fuel tank system. The undercarriage was very "stalk-like" and apt to collapse if a heavy landing took place, and in this connection Ginger suffered his humiliation.

We had completed our familiarisation flights with an Instructor and were at full strength as a bomber crew (7) with the addition of Joe Hatter from Essex as Flight Engineer and Alan (Al) Applegath , a Canadian volunteer from Vancouver, as gunner (mid-upper turret). We were now on our own doing circuits and landings, and rarely got a bad landing from Ginger, but on this attempt he excelled himself. The aircraft lost flying speed too high above the runway, and dropped like a falling brick wall -thump! Up in the air on the rebound; the drill in those circumstances was to open up and go round again, Ginger thought otherwise.

Down we thumped, to rise even higher than before, or so it seemed to me sitting in the second pilot's seat. So it continued down the runway - thump - bang - thump - on what was reputed to be the shakiest designed undercarriage in service.

We stopped eventually, and avoided running off the end of the runway, Ginger's face ruddy and glistening with perspiration The rest of us were very quiet until the silence was broken by a very curt voice from the watch-tower requesting Pilot Officer Guy to report to the Commanding Officer immediately. The aircraft was grounded for a complete inspection of the undercarriage, and fortunately for Ginger no damage could be found, although he was given a verbal sorting out on how to land a Stirling. His troubles at Wigsley did not end there, for on two occasions we had to return to Base before completing our exercise.

Once it was due to engines losing power and the other time some faulty equipment, which decided to play up in the middle of a thunder storm. The C.O. called Ginger, Vic and myself, into his office and seemed to think that we should have pressed on through the bad weather, holding Ginger responsible for deciding to return. No doubt the C.O. was under pressure to get the crews trained at any cost, for losses in the operational squadrons were high, but Ginger was a sensible pilot and stuck by his own decisions - better safe, than down on a training flight.

Just how serious the losses on ops were, was brought home to us a month later. We were now at No, 5 Lancaster Finishing School (L.F.S.) at Syerston near Nottingham, on the last lap of our training - converting from Stirlings to Lancasters. We were in the Officers Mess one afternoon at tea time when the conversation and rattle of tea cups were abruptly silenced as the radio news announcer reported 94 aircraft lost the previous night on a raid to Nuremberg.

The pause in the conversation underlined the impact of the announcement - we all knew it couldn't possibly happen to us, and yet...................

We went into Nottingham as often as we could, it was a friendly city, certainly the girls were! The two hotels we frequented were the Flying Horse (known as the airborne nag) and The Black Swan (known as the mucky duck). Our problem with the fair sex was the Yanks, for they had plenty of money and were more direct in their approach to women. Most of the Yanks, did not leave much doubt as to what they expected, and since their casualties in the Flying Fortresses were high, perhaps they did not have much time for courtship! Some (not all) of the girls were put off by this 'chat-up line', and we enjoyed their company on the rebound.

One evening, on the bus returning to camp, a Sergeant Air Gunner boarded and stood in the aisle, gazing at the rest of us with an alcoholic leer. 'Oh you poor bastards ' he said, 'you will soon be seeing the Happy Valley (the Ruhr) and God help you all'. He did not appreciate that he was one of the lucky ones who had survived.

The Lancasters we flew at L.F.S. were retired veterans as were most of the aircraft used in training; when we did our evasive corkscrewing manoeuvre we had to watch that certain speeds and stresses were not exceeded, Pieces were likely to fall off -such as the wings! We had an aged Hurricane fighter in full pursuit for our gunners to aim at, but we had to wait whilst the fighter gained height and dived down on us, getting sufficient speed to simulate an attack. (Post war accounts from German fighter pilots stated that they attacked the Lancaster from underneath, firing up!) We did appreciate how much better the Lancaster was in performance than any of the other aircraft we flew in, and after our two months of conversion training we were sent on a week's leave, prior to a posting to an operational Squadron. It was April 1944.

East Kirkby

No. 57 Squadron was based at East Kirkby near Boston, Lincolnshire, part of 5 group the airfield had been constructed on flat farmland like many other wartime fields, with a brick built watchtower surrounded by Nissen huts. These huts were scattered and dispersed among the fields surrounding the airfield, some for sleeping accommodation, others as messes and ablutions; the larger ones used for briefing rooms and flight offices. They even had ammunition and incendiary bombs stacked up in the larger type Nissens.

The watchtower presided over two squadrons of Lancasters (57 and 630) dispersed around the airfield. Each aircraft had its own concrete hard standing off this perimeter track (peri-track, as it was called..)

The main and longest runway ran roughly East to West, the only hazard being a hill (there are some in the wilds of Lincolnshire) at the Eastern end , which needed watching when staggering off with a full bomb and petrol load. In the middle of the airfield stood a deserted farmhouse, oblivious to the continuous activity of men and machines, yet it seemed to me to be waiting patiently for us all to stop messing about and let it return to its proper use.

Lancaster over East Kirkby

The Lancasters of 57 Squadron bore the code letters DX and an alphabetical letter for each aircraft. They were equipped with the latest Rolls Royce Merlin Engines and the latest navigational aids that included H2S. This was a code name for an airborne scanner mounted in a pod below the mid-upper gun turret; the screen and operational equipment was situated on the right hand side of the Navigators table. The scanner, rotating through 360° in its pod, sent out a pulse that was reflected back from the ground and shown on the screen. Roofs and buildings in towns reflected well and showed up clearly, whereas water did not, thus the outline of rivers and coast lines stood out. One had a picture of the ground, with the towns showing as larger white areas and even showing their individual shape.

In 5 Group the Air Bomber sat alongside the Navigator operating this equipment and giving him fixes of the aircraft's position for his plotting chart. On the Navigator's left was the Gee Set, which was another radar set, operated by receiving signals from different ground stations and showing these on a screen. By plotting these signals on a special chart one could pinpoint the exact position of the aircraft. This Gee equipment had been in use for some years and the Germans had set up a comprehensive jamming system so that beyond our own coast it rapidly became useless. We were assured that the Pulses sent out by our H2S equipment were not being used by the Germans to track us; based on the fact that losses were as many with aircraft not carrying H2S as those that were. (Rather a negative approach; in fact post-war investigation revealed that the Germans "homed in" on the Bomber stream using the H2S transmissions on their search radar).

Ginger Guy was sent off on a "second dickey" trip - a reference to the spare dickey seat of the old cars - whereby he flew with an experienced crew for his first "op" as second pilot to see what it was all about. We waited, with some anxiety, for his return from Munich, because one of the crews who had come all the way through training with us lost their pilot on his first "experience" sortie. Not only did they lose a friend and pilot, but also they had to return to Conversion Unit and crew up again.

Ginger survived, however, and the day after his return we were briefed for our first night operation - the target, an aircraft works on an airfield at Clermont Ferrand in France. Opposition would be negligible, we were told, bombing would take place from 4000! This turned out to be a standard height for attacking targets in France, no doubt it improved the accuracy of the bombing but it exposed us to heavier A.A. fire from the ground. Night fighters looking for us did not have to climb far, and on moonlit nights with low cloud we were readily visible. Ours not to reason why, however, and apart from our first-time nerves the trip was quiet and in the moonlight I could see clearly the hangers of the airfield as we bombed.

Our second sortie was to a factory making aircraft parts at Tours and as we crossed the French coast and roared across the dark countryside I wondered about the people on the ground, were they saying "good luck" or more likely "don't drop anything here". One group of people was positive, the German A.A. gunners hosed the air, with tracer bullets flashing-past us, and their message was pointed. The target was marked by our own 5 Group Pathfinders who, in theory, reached the target ahead of the Main Force, dropped flares and marked with red incendiaries called "spot fires". On this occasion they had put the red spots in the right place, as we could see clearly from our low height of 4000', and I could easily identify the aiming point for our load of 18 x 500lb bombs dropped as a stick. This was not as difficult as it sounds. An electric switch controlled the release mechanism for each bomb. In my compartment in the nose of the aircraft was a rotary switch, (nicknamed Mickey Mouse) which started at position 1 when the bomb release button was pushed, and went on quickly to all the other contacts one by one, until all the bombs were gone.

We used the Navigation aids, plus radio fixes from the Wireless Operator, astro navigation (star fixes) very rarely and visual map reading when conditions permitted, between them we did not go astray too far. I would sit alongside Vic at the Navigators table and use the H2S until approaching the target, then go forward into the nose of the Lanc for the run up and bombing of the target.

When we had cleared the target area I would return to the table unless at any time there was enemy fighter activity which necessitated my stopping in the front turret, (armed with two .303 machine guns) which was above the Air Bomber's position in the nose of the aircraft. There was no need for me to man these twin Browning machine guns all the time, as the Pilot and Flight Engineer scanned the area forward, whilst the Mid-Upper and Rear Gunner covered the area behind.

Mailly Le Camp

We were briefed for an attack on a German military base and tank park at Mailly Le Camp in France. It was a brilliant moonlit night, the period of full moon had not yet passed and we were flying on our 3rd operation in 4 nights. In at the deep end with a vengeance!! We were due to be in the first wave of the attack but there was a delay in the marking, so we were ordered to circle the area whilst the Pathfinders sorted things out. The 'Master Bomber' was Group Captain Cheshire on this op, flying in a Mosquito Fighter/Bomber at low level to assess their efforts.

Mailly le Camp, before

He couldn't have been much lower than us, at our usual 4000', and circling around was very dangerous indeed, not only were the German night fighters around, but the risk of collision with 300 aircraft circling was high. Aircraft were exploding on the ground, and in the air; as two collided there was a large explosion, and fiery pieces fell to earth like molten wax dripping from a candle, (they were probably Pathfinder aircraft carrying flares).

48

I was checking over the bombsight and selector switches, waiting to go in and attack, when I saw another Lancaster head on - coming straight at us. There was no time to shout a warning, nor do anything except duck instinctively, fortunately the other aircraft thundered overhead leaving us all shattered, and I do not think it did anything for the nerves of the other crew either.

Eventually, we were ordered in, and I could see clearly the hutted camp that was our target and some trenches alongside, either gun emplacements or air raid shelters. My bombs went down and then the whole area was obliterated by smoke and explosions as the rest of the force dropped their loads, nobody was keen on waiting around any longer. Our losses that night were high (42 aircraft out of a total of 338) but the attack was very successful; it was the beginning of May 1944 and every blow at German men and equipment was a help to the Second Front.

Mailly le Camp, after

We guessed that this was not far off, for on a map in the Briefing Room there was a large slice of South-East England ruled off with the words "Down here do not go" written across it. I suspect that "Security" had laid down the ban, but we would never have gone into that area, trigger-happy troops down there would have shot at anything.

Because of this, however, our routes to France were directed from Lincolnshire, across country to the South Coast around Plymouth, and from there across the Channel into Northern France, thus avoiding all our

South and East Coast from the Wash round to Portland Bill

Two nights later we attacked the airfield at Tours, still in the bright moonlight, and for us the trip was uneventful; odd spots of flak and no sign of fighters, or so we thought. Two aircraft from our Squadron on the same attack were missing, however, and the crew of one of them turned up later, having been shot up twice by fighters and crash landing at an airfield in the South of England.

Springtime in England in 1944 was like many other years, the promise of fine weather soon turned to rain and cloud. Several operations planned during the day had to be cancelled due to bad weather over the target that night. We were often briefed, had a meal, collected our kit and transported out to the aircraft, there to await take-off and then the whole thing would be cancelled. This was notified to us at our dispersal points by firing a coloured ' Very ' light from the Watch-Tower, and as it fizzed in the air one could hear cheers all round the airfield.

The cheers were a reaction to the tension generated in getting ready to do another trip, usually when an op was "scrubbed" like this it was too late to go anywhere but into the mess and unwind with a pint. Hilarious parties resulted with such events as rugby matches across the furniture (Senior officers always seemed to get at the bottom of heaps of players), chair stacking, and upside down walking on the ceiling. "Line shooting" took place at any time and was likely to break out whenever a group of flyers were gathered around the bar. The "line" was some extravagant statement made to impress everybody, usually about our flying activity, but very humorous in its content. An example, that I heard, was from a certain Flying Officer who said "My bombing is so accurate I aim at the fences round the railway marshalling yards to let the saboteurs in".

Tension could show itself in several ways; the "twitch" was perhaps the most common, the sufferer would be unaware that he had developed a nervous tic of some kind - an eyelid blink or a muscle spasm. He was left unaware, because everybody was sympathetic and " there but for the Grace of God go I". It was left to the Medical Officer to be diplomatic and if things got too bad he would get the sufferer posted, before he went L.M.F. This "Lack of Moral Fibre" label was the official name for a coward, and the thought of being branded as such was more daunting than going on "ops"; there was a limit, however, and some men reached the limit quicker than others. Bad experiences, like being shot up, crew members killed, friends killed or missing, nightmares and homes bombed were not good preparation for another sortie, enough to give anybody the "twitch".

Around this time it was decided that because the French trips were 'easy' that the number of ops in a tour would be increased to 35, some reports said 45. Casualties, however, were no less than in the preceding months, and the whole idea was dropped. On our Squadron, we were not even advised of the proposal, no crew had lasted 30 trips for long enough.

Our next trip was to the railway marshalling yards at Amiens. It was stressed that accuracy was important as the yards were near the centre of the town and built up area, we would get no credit for bombing French houses, the inhabitants wouldn't like it. We were on time at the target, but the clouds were low and the weather atrocious, the Pathfinders were late, obviously having trouble in finding the target. We descended through the cloud, not a pleasant experience at any time, and came out over the target, which was lit up like fairyland by flares, dropped by the Pathfinders. Fortunately, they had just marked the target, and we were ordered in. I could see the railway tracks very clearly in the light of the flares reflected from the black clouds above, and we were quick to drop our load and turn for home. The bright lights were not for us, I may have been able to see the target but we felt exposed and vulnerable to fighter attack silhouetted against the clouds.

The local pub in the village of East Kirkby was 'The Red Lion' and on non-operational nights it was very busy. Rather than fight our way through the crush, four of us in the crew, Ginger, Vic, Al, and myself clubbed together to buy an old 'banger', a Morris 10. For servicing, we left the car with the ground crew on the aircraft dispersal, when we went off on ops. They had the use of it while we were away, and looked after it mechanically, I think it had as much care as our Lancaster.

We used to go off to Skegness or Boston as often as we could, petrol was rationed, but we had a sympathetic Garage owner in a nearby village, who helped out when we ran short. Al taught me to drive, luckily there were not many other motorists about to observe my mistakes. We did meet a herd of cattle head on in the narrow main street of Boston, I stopped and the cattle literally walked all over us, bending one headlight. It was in Boston, at a dance at the Assembly Rooms, that I first met Iris, an attractive nurse, who put up with my two left feet and broken dates, when I had to fly. Her parents ran a fish and chip shop, which also endeared her to me, they were very kind to servicemen, and frequently served them late into the night after the pubs had closed.

The crew had a week's leave and as Ginger would not have been able to get home to Wales and back in time, he came home with me to Pinner. We went up to Town and saw the sights, Ginger used a unique chat-up line under the statue of Eros(boarded up for the duration). He approached two Wrens and asked them whether they were lost!. I left him around midnight , still talking with one of the Wrens. He missed the last train, hitch-hiked and walked back to Pinner, finding his way to my home by instinct I guess.

One of the routine jobs for Bomber Command was mining and our 6th sortie was a marathon solo flight, mine laying in Kiel Bay. The area in which we were to lay the mines was used for U-boat training and our H2S navigational aid was used to its best advantage to ensure we dropped them in the right place. With the H2S it was easy to find a pinpoint on an island in the bay, the land stood out so clearly on the picture tube.

We flew a set course at 20000' dropping the mines at regular intervals; each mine had its own parachute and was activated after it had sunk into the water. All went well, until we turned West for home.

The picture on the H2S tube showed that the heading we were flying was towards Russia and the East, the compass was also suspect, gyrating wildly, so we altered course 90° to the North. This made no difference to our picture on the H2S, so we decided that it had gone U/S (unserviceable) and turned on an average westerly reading on the compass. We descended as we went and the problem resolved itself, the rotary scanner had frozen up pointing East, and as we lost height, freed itself; even the compass settled down. It must have been a cold night over Kiel Bay

The Fatherland itself was not to be deprived of our attentions and the night after our long trip to Kiel, operation No.7. was to Brunswick. Low lying cloud and misty conditions delayed the Pathfinders, and had us circling around again awaiting instructions, a new technique for bombing was being tried out. Previous attacks had been so accurate that the markers had been bombed out of existence almost as soon as they had been laid, leaving nothing for a proportion of the main force to aim at.

The new idea was to lay the markers away from the target, and set a false wind reading on the bombsight, which would allow for the marker being in the wrong place. Thus we would aim at the marker but the false setting on the bombsight would cause the bombs to fall on the required target! The false setting was due to be worked out by the Pathfinders, and passed to us via the Master Bomber, hence the delays and our circling around, whilst the calculations were done.

Nerves got a bit frayed and in the distance we could see some poor devil coned in a dozen searchlights or more and desperately trying to get clear. Radio silence was supposed to be absolute, we were all waiting for the instructions, when a plaintive Australian voice came on the air "We want to go home" and got a very short answer from the Master Bomber. We stooged about Germany for far too long and bombed through the murk as instructed; as we turned away we could hear the Master Bomber giving fresh instructions; it appeared we had been attacking a dummy target. I expect that some of the more experienced crews found the right target but at that stage we did as we were ordered.

Towards the end of May the crescendo of attacks on tactical targets increased prior to the invasion. On the 24th we attacked the docks at Antwerp (Op No. 8), not a long flight, but a well-defended target. The radio frequency we were using to listen for instructions from the Master Bomber was picking up the B.B.C. programme, so that the run up to the target was enlivened by a song amidst the thump of exploding A.A. shells. My instructions to Ginger to 'open bomb door' 'steady' and 'bombs gone' were interspersed with Peter Dawson singing, 'Old Father Thames goes rolling along down to the mighty sea"!

I thought to myself that I'd rather be at home listening to the B.B.C. than being shot at!

From May 27th to June 5th we were on 4 more sorties attacking railways yards and gun emplacements on the French Coast. During this period the Germans were sending over 'Intruder' aircraft to shoot down our Lancs as they came in to land after an op. At other times they came over as we were waiting to take off. On a particularly wet night we were taxying out on the perimeter track heading for the Take-off point, when all the lights on the airfield went out. We remained with our engines running, and a small van came along carrying the C.O. His orders were not to shoot at any Intruder, in case the tracer revealed the airfield. We heard an aircraft passing over but due to the low rainy clouds we could not see it, better still he could not see us! Strict orders had been given also to the A.A. gunners not to fire so we waited patiently for permission to move on.

As the sound of engines died away overhead, the lights came on revealing a flooded runway. A solitary Lancaster stood on the threshold awaiting take-off. Over the R/T came the gentlemanly voice of S/Leader D.R. Wyness, * known as the 'Duke'. "May I scramble from the shambles, "he said. Nobody answered, but he was given a green light from the control Caravan at the end of the runway. The show went on.!

* Later on S/Ldr Wyness moved to 617 Squadron, was shot down and handed over to the Gestapo, who executed him.

Over the English Channel on the night of June 5th there was low cloud cover. The gun emplacement we bombed was only visible to us as a red glow from the marker spot fire. There were 100 aircraft in the attack so that the whole area was covered, if the target markers were accurate the guns were saturated. In the short time that we had been operating, the techniques used in marking the targets had improved, more Mosquito fighter/bombers were used to seek out the target by the light of flares, dropped from a special Lancaster Flare Force. Experienced pilots put down the 'spot' fires', if they were in the right place extra marking was carried out. If they were wrong a different colour was used, and the Main Force instructed accordingly. No doubt the guns we bombed on June 5th had been marked from very low level, because the cloud cover was at 2000'. This meant that on our way back across the Channel we could not see the invasion fleet visually, but we did see them on our H2S radar screen, so many white blobs that we thought at first the equipment was faulty.

On the night of D-Day itself - the 6th - we were over Caen bombing the bridges, for No. 5 Group had been allocated to support bombing for the invasion troops. Our targets in the following fortnight were in close support, often small villages where German forces were assembling, tank parks and railway sidings. The tonnage of bombs falling on some of those "villages", not to mention the artillery fire by day, reduced them to rubble; if the inhabitants had not fled, they were not left much to salvage.

We were returning from one such sortie across the English Channel when Taffy, the Rear Gunner, came up on the intercom to direct our attention to the large number of lights or objects that were fairly nipping along above the water. What is more, they were being shot at, as the lines of tracer bullets showed. All was revealed the next day, they were the first V.1. flying bombs on their way to London.

By 21st June we had completed 17 operations; flown through much A.A. fire, seen many aircraft on fire - both in the air and on the ground - yet a night fighter had not attacked us, nor had we been hit by flak; this was to change.

Wesseling

On the night of 21st June 1944 we were briefed for a raid on Wesseling, a town on the Rhine between Cologne and Bonn. Our target was a synthetic petrol plant, the attack, part of a joint campaign with the U.S.A.A.F. against oil targets, a campaign which continued throughout the war. We had no particular premonition that this flight would be different from all the others, the target was only on the German border and the short night precluded long hours over enemy territory.

We parted from our ground crew with the usual good wishes from them; they used to watch me checking out the bomb loads, with good humour, often telling me not bring them back. They took a pride in our aircraft 'L' for Love - which was new and had only been flown on operations by us, we expected to be airborne and return in about 4 1/2 hours. We were due to go on leave the following week, so we were looking forward to that. Having survived so far, Ginger was in line for promotion to flight Commander; (Acting F/Lt), casualties on operational squadrons meant rapid promotion for the remainder.

We were soon climbing up to our operational height for this sortie - 19,000', along with many other aircraft. From the ground we all looked like midges against the evening sky, apparently flying in different directions and droning away as we gained height. At 00.30 hours on the morning of the 22nd we set course across Norfolk, Vic & I operating the Gee and H2S and out across the North Sea, altering course for the target soon after passing the Dutch Coast.

We were approaching Eindhoven and could see several aircraft shot down and burning on the ground ahead, so we turned for a few moments to avoid flying directly over Eindhoven. Taffy usually reported aircraft crashes to Vic ,the navigator, to record the time in the log, but there were so many it was not possible.

As we regained our normal course there was an enormous explosion alongside the aircraft. The flash and impact came together and the aircraft lurched over to port, small flames flickered down the inside of the fuselage, which I can only assume were the electrical wires shorting out. "We've been hit, " said Ginger and the glow from outside illuminated his face and that of Joe Hatter the Engineer sat beside him. The engines were running OK and nobody in the crew reported being injured, but Ginger rapidly made his decision and gave the' order "Put on Parachutes".

My 'chute was kept in the Air Bombers compartment in the nose so I unplugged my intercom and went forward from the Navigators table, glancing out at the starboard wing as I went. The petrol tanks had been ruptured, and the flames from the burning wing reached back beyond the rear turret; the rush of air was sucking the petrol out of the tanks and fuelling the flames like a blowtorch. I could see that the wing itself would not last long. For a moment I thought that if the aircraft exploded, like so many we had seen, I was going to die, and felt sad that I would not see my home again.

A feeling of great calm settled over me, a wonderful sensation of peace, unlike anything I had experienced before, or since. I like to think that many of the aircrew who died, trapped in their aircraft, also felt this absolute peace, 'that passeth all understanding'.

My training took over and as smoke filled the plane I crawled into the nose where I plugged in my intercom. Clipping on my parachute, I heard Ginger give the order to bale out (Jump Jump), saying that he could not control the aircraft much longer. I could see him watching as Joe and I jettisoned the front hatch, which was part of the floor. The escape drill was that I went first, followed by Joe, with Vic behind him. The two gunners and the Wireless Operator went out through the rear door and the pilot with his seat parachute left via the top canopy above his head.

I rolled myself into a ball and left the aircraft; the slipstream caught at me, but I fell clear and was surprised to find that I could think quite clearly. I had expected to be muddled and jumbled in my thoughts but I suppose the extra adrenaline gave me a, stimulus. I counted the number of times I turned head over heels (three) before I fell towards the darkness that was the 'deck'. The noise of the engines still rang in my ears, although I must have been well clear of the aircraft, but to make sure I let myself fall. I became aware that the stars were at my feet, so I was falling head first, no blacking-out sensation; and I was facing the horizon which showed itself as a thin streak of light - I was looking to the North. It was a very pleasant feeling dropping through space and the thought came that it seemed so unreal, that if I was dead it wasn't so bad after all.

I knew I had plenty of space below, we were flying at 19000' when we were hit , but I decided to try my 'chute. This was attached to a harness and clipped on my chest, opened by pulling a 'D' shaped ring on the front. I grabbed this and moved my arm from across my chest to the outstretched position; I wouldn't say I pulled it, just a movement, but it produced results very quickly.

Something snicked past my face and there was a hefty jerk, which stopped me in mid-air, right way up, before I could blink, it was most sudden The straps above were pinning my head, not uncomfortably, but in such a way that I couldn't twist my head to look behind. Somewhere below me, an aircraft, probably my own, exploded on hitting the ground and the bright glow illuminated the sky making me feel very visible and vulnerable.

The only signs that showed I was still falling were the wind whining through the rigging lines of the 'chute and the swaying movement that became violent at times and caused me to retch. I stretched up and tugged on the lines each time I swayed, and this eased things considerably, reducing the swinging. All became very quiet, there were little twinkles of flak bursts in the distance and from different points of the compass a red glow on the ground where aircraft had crashed.

Although it didn't seem very long since I had baled out, I must have been in the air for a long time; the fact that it was quiet meant that the rest of the aircraft had gone on to the target. I could not see the ground, for there was a low bank of cloud which I thought would be at about 2,000', the same as the cloud base over England, which we had left not so long ago.

Once I had gone through this I could expect to be on the ground almost immediately, and as I dropped into the grey mist I drew my legs up and waited for it to clear. Beneath the cloud it was very dark and I could see nothing; the first intimation that I was anywhere near solid earth was a crackling noise and some leaves brushing my face. A gentle bump and I touched the ground still in the approved "sitting" position for landing, very surprised at being down and in one piece.

I stood up, looked around at the trees and then up at my 'chute which had collapsed over four or five of the small pine trees in this forest. Our evaders instructions were to bury the 'chute to avoid detection, but there was no way I could get that 'chute down, so I unbuckled my harness and left 'chute and harness dangling in the tree; the sooner I was on my way the better.

My emotions were very mixed, we had been told that even strong men wept at the sound of the other aircraft returning without them; they were not my sentiments at all. I was truly glad to be alive and not injured; out of the burning aircraft and not part of the many wrecks I had seen on the way down.

I opened my aids box, which was issued prior to every flight, it contained, among other things, maps, money in different currencies, a compass and Horlicks tablets. By the light of a gun flash in the distance I saw a narrow path through the woods, leading off in what I thought was the right direction. I checked it with the compass and started walking due West carrying my life jacket ("Mae West") under my arm. I walked for about 20 minutes with the planes flying above me, for they were now returning from the target. I could see the flash of the A.A. guns and hear the shells bursting high above the cloud layer, and as I listened one of our aircraft was hit and I could hear it whistling down, to break cloud about 3 miles ahead of me, flaming from nose to tail. The light from the explosion lit up the whole wood where I was standing and I expected to be challenged at any minute.

That finished my walk to the West, there would be German troops at the scene of the crash, so I turned South at the next fork in the path. I had travelled for a further 20 minutes before a peculiar shape loomed up in the darkness, which made me flatten out on the ground immediately. It was a high pyramid-shaped pile with a box-shaped section running up one side and off the top; and in my imagination it looked like one of the launching sites for V1 rockets, pictures of which had been issued only a few days earlier. I reasoned that if it was a V1 site there would be many troops around, so I must avoid the area at all costs.

I found a track which took me away from the site and soon came across a single-track railway line leading away from the pile, which seemed to confirm my suspicions, although there was no sound of military activity.

(If I had approached closer I would have found that it was a railway line leading to a slagheap from the local coal mine! In my tensed up state, every bush was a menace.)

If there were any troops in the area, likely to use the railway, it was obviously not safe for me, so I turned off through the woods up a hill, still trying, with the aid of the compass, to head South West. When I reached the top of the hill I could see four aircraft burning on the ground in the distance, and soon after a belt of trees gave way to some open ground with corn fields; below in the valley were 2 houses close together. I retreated into the trees and as it was breaking dawn (the shortest night of

58

the year was over) I decided to stay in the woods and observe the houses for the following day, to see if any Germans went near them.

After burying my Mae West I hid under some bushes and settled down to sleep for a couple of hours. When the cold of the early morning brought me awake I ate two Horlicks tablets from the aids box and decided to ration the rest out at 2 for every 6 hours. The houses I was watching were part of a farm and the workers started early, leaving the immediate vicinity. I was some distance away and felt that a closer look was warranted. To avoid being seen and to eliminate as much noise as possible, I crawled on my hands and knees with plenty of rest periods. I kept out of view of the houses within the cover of the wood, and I could hear traffic on a road in the vicinity. I must have been crawling parallel to it, for although I heard traffic all day, I did not find it. I would have liked to reach a point where I could have observed the road to ascertain whether the Germans used it often, the noise of the traffic certainly seemed to indicate so. All I found were "fire breaks" in the forest, sandy tracks, across which I scuttled like a rabbit to avoid being seen, and often in the company of the aforesaid animal.

When the sun was warm enough I slept some more, then stayed on the edge of a small clearing watching the farm and workers until it finally became dark at 11.30 P.M. Nobody went near the houses all day, although they looked occupied and as I approached them I reckoned I had two options. The first was to obtain help if they happened to be part of the underground organisation; if not I needed water and an exact idea of my place on the map. If they were part of the underground resistance I would be very lucky, for although we knew such people existed, we had no idea who they were nor how to contact them. I walked round the back of the first house and hammered on the back door - no reply I went over to the other house and repeated the knocking on the other back door. No luck either. I could see the upstairs windows were open, so assuming the occupants of the house had retired to bed I threw a handful of grit through the window giving a cautious shout of "oy". No sign of life at all and I was about to leave when I heard a footstep on the path leading to the other house. I nipped back smartly to the first door and probably gave the farm worker standing there a nasty shock, for grabbing his arm I pushed him into his own house muttering in German " Ich bin Englisch" .

Without answering, he pulled the blinds, put on the lights and could see I was dressed in my blue uniform with flying boots. I showed him my maps and asked him to tell me where I had landed, expecting him to say

"Holland", To my surprise he said I was in Belgium, in Lanklaer Wood, on the Holland / Belgium border about halfway between the towns of Maastricht and Masaeyk; I had landed and walked further South than I had thought. He filled my water bottle (also part of the escape aids box) gave me some milk and by sign language and a few words in German, told me that I mustn't tell anybody, because he could be shot for helping me.

I asked him what I ought to do, giving him every opportunity to tell me if he knew of any evaders organisation, but as he only shrugged his shoulders, I knew he could not, or would not, help.

Lanklaer Wood

From studying the map I decided to head South West towards Hasselt, it was a fair sized town and in the right direction; it might have some Resistance contacts. The snag was, that the nights were so short that I would not be able to get far each night and I would have to ask at other farms for food and water. With luck I might contact a helpful organisation in the process. I parted from the farmhand with many thanks, and marched off at a brisk pace covering 3 or 4 miles before crossing a railway, then some bumpy fields. I was passing through a copse of trees when I saw the headlights of a car on the road ahead. I let it pass, crossed the road quickly only to find a ploughed field, which made for heavy going. I came across an old mill and walked over to have a look; and as I stepped on to the path leading to the mill, my feet crunched on the gravel like the noise of a dozen men. It looked deserted and I was surprised to see a man step out of a hut near the mill; he had apparently heard my footsteps but was unable to see me as I stood still in the shadow. He was in civilian clothes and looked like a caretaker;. After looking around he re-entered the hut and as he appeared to be alone I walked up to the door and stepped inside, where he was seated by the stove.

He didn't seem surprised to see me, and was, I thought, pleased to have someone to talk to. He was suspicious at first (as everybody turned out to be) but after we had been talking a short while, mostly in sign language and odd words of German, he offered me some of his cold coffee which I drank with relish. I asked him who worked at the mill, hoping for a contact with the Resistance, but he said they were mixed, some good, some bad. "Were there many Germans in the area?" I asked, and his answer was depressing for he said that there were about 500 stationed in each village around. That afternoon a German Officer and six armed men had called at the mill searching for English airmen If I could get to the village where he lived, he went on to say, he knew people there who had already assisted English flyers, his house was at Rothem about 15 kilometres to the North. He couldn't leave the mill immediately, so he drew me a diagram on the table with a piece of chalk, how to get to a place in the woods where he would meet me the following morning.

My objective was a deserted house with a red roof, originally a German strong point, but now disused. I was to wait there until 7 o'clock; he would come and take me to his own house at Rothem. I had to cross a road, a railway, and then another road, keeping parallel to the last road and moving through the forest until I came to the house with a red roof, which was opposite 5 tall chimneys.

All this seemed clear enough from his sketch map on the table, although it meant retracing my steps. It was all in the wrong direction; that is, to the North instead of my escape direction South West. Nevertheless, I reasoned that I must make contact with some organised group and if that meant going off' in the wrong direction so be it.

I started out, crossed the road, railway and the other road, as planned, and kept parallel with the road, keeping to the fields and forest; so far, so good. The going became very rough and progress was so slow, that I stepped back on to the grass verge of the road and marched along there, keeping a very wary eye open for cyclists or patrols of any sort. I walked on and on, searching for the 5 chimneys. I could not find them, and it became dangerous for me to continue, because daylight had come and the time was already 5.30 A.M.

I thought it prudent to get back into the woods bordering the road, to wait there, and watch for the caretaker of the mill passing on his way home. I had just got clear of the road and in the bushes, crashing about, when a gendarme cycled by, luckily he didn't stop or even look in my direction; I didn't move much after that and kept under cover. Several cyclists passed by, but my watchman was not among them so about 7.30 A.M. I gave up looking, and retired deeper into the wood. I searched until I found a hollow filled with dead leaves and slept there until 10 A. M., when the cold brought me awake, shivering. A typically English mid-summer day set in, fine drizzle and an icy wind; I needed to find some shelter for the day; It had been arranged with the watchman that if I couldn't make our rendezvous that morning I would be there the next.

There was a red roofed building nearby in the wood, which I thought may be the one I was trying to reach, although there was no sign of the chimneys. This wishful thinking was put aside, for as I approached the path leading to the house I could read the board at the entrance. BADHAUS it proclaimed, not a deserted German strong point but a

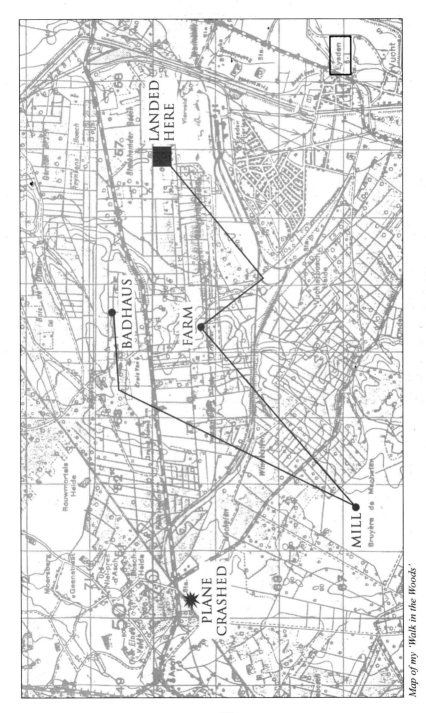

Map of my 'Walk in the Woods'

63

BATH HOUSE, more likely they came here by the lorry load for their ablutions!

There were two labourers working nearby, within a barbed wire perimeter fence; they had seen me approach on the path, so I went over to ask them about the five chimneys I was seeking. They stopped digging and came over to the wire and I could see they were discussing my uniform. I explained that I was an English airman who had been shot down the night before last and was trying to get to Rothem where I had been promised help.

I asked if there were many Germans in the district and were they likely to come to this Badhaus? "No", they said, "not many come to the Badhaus", but there were German troops all over the place, and especially at Rothem, they certainly wouldn't recommend me to go there!

One of them asked me whether I had eaten, and when told that it was two nights ago, gave me an egg sandwich. The egg was heavily salted and the bread was like eating dry compressed bran, but I was too hungry to care and felt better for eating something solid.

I was preparing to leave and thanking them for their information, when the man who had given me the sandwich said that if I went to the house nearby, which was the home of the Badhaus caretaker, the caretaker's wife would give me a meal. He must have seen how I had wolfed his sandwich!

That sounded good to me so I went up to the house, or small shack as it turned out to be, just two bare rooms on the ground floor. My luck had taken a turn for the better, for as soon as I had explained to the wife who I was, she called to her husband and he became very excited, pumping my hand and ordering his son to go off and fetch somebody else. Whilst his wife prepared a couple of eggs for me, I asked him if he knew the people who helped English airmen, and was elated to hear him say that he did, and that I would be back in England within a week. I couldn't see how, but I was very content to believe it.

The caretaker produced a razor and I had my first wash and saw my face in the mirror.

I was quite a sight. I had a heavy stubble matted with dirt, mixed with blood from a cut above my lip, of which I had been totally unaware. I could only assume it had been caused by the parachute as it opened, or the metal hooks to which the 'chute was attached. I felt much better after the wash and shave and the caretaker told me that a Canadian airman had been caught nearby, the same night that I had landed. The Gendarmes had found him and handed him over to the Germans; he did not know his name, but from his description it sounded like our mid-upper Gunner, Al Applegath. A large number of aircraft had crashed, however, and most crews had a Canadian among them; I hoped Al was still on the run.

When I had finished the meal the caretaker took me to a hiding place in the grounds of the Badhaus. It was a carefully prepared dug-out, boarded up inside, with a flap that closed over the entrance, which was then covered by bushes making it invisible from a distance. He'd put some straw inside with a couple of cushions and as it was pitch black I soon fell asleep. 1 do not know how long I slept, but came awake as the flap lifted and the caretaker dropped in with another man, who he introduced as Toon. (Antoon or Anthony in English).

'Toon' (Antoon Gielen) White Brigade Commander in 1949

He was the man the caretaker's son had been sent to find and was the leader of the local "White Brigade" resistance group, this was all he would say at the time

He took my name, rank and number and said that he would return later with some civilian clothes, after my credentials had been checked with London, so that my relatives would know that I was alive. That was good news, so I went back to sleep, quite happy, oblivious of the fact that if my particulars didn't check out, Toon would put a bullet through me, he had a short way with traitors, or German infiltrators. My stumbling German conversation did not help either. Toon was Flemish and spoke little German, or English for that matter!

He returned later that afternoon, however, with a blue coat, black pullover and black trousers. I cut off the legging part of my flying boots, using the special knife kept in the side of the boot for that very purpose. This left the appearance of a pair of shoes, but they were fleecy lined and a bit too warm for hiking about. With an old scarf to hide my blue R. A. F. shirt and a cloth cap I was ready to leave on the bicycle Toon had brought with him.

I thanked the caretaker and his wife and mounting the bike rode off.

Not very far, because it had a back pedalling brake (fixed wheel) and no other brakes at all. I tried to free wheel to ask where the brakes were and flew straight over the handlebars. I found out! I suppose we should all have been pleased that I could ride a bike at all, nobody asked.

We cycled back down the path, then out on to the road; I remembered to cycle on the right hand side of the road but felt self-conscious and conspicuous. On we went through a small village, then past a large building which was the offices for the local coal mine, although I was not aware of this at the time. The slagheap I had seen on the first night was part of this mine.

As we passed this building a German soldier came by, with his rifle slung over his shoulder, he gave us both a glance and walked on. He was the first soldier I had seen close up, and I realised that I couldn't have been as conspicuous as I felt, however I would be glad to get to our destination.

Eisden

We came, finally, to a small town (Eisden) with many German troops moving about and Toon led me into a Cafe in the main street. This was Toon's home, his parents ran the Cafe and he had identity cards to prove himself a miner, he did no work now except for the Resistance, which kept him busy. I discovered later that his mining "connections" supplied dynamite to help with the sabotage.

I was hidden upstairs in a bedroom until evening and then I joined Toon and his father in the living room to listen to the news from England. His father had worked in Germany at some time and was able to understand my broken German better than his son, both our conversations improved as the evening went on, and the cognac flowed.

The following morning I was introduced to Bob, an English wireless operator, who was in contact with London, who also had the job of checking up on people like myself to see whether they were genuine. The Germans had a habit of infiltrating the Resistance groups by using captured uniforms and identity discs to try to pass off one of their own men as an evader. Bob's method of interrogation was to ask me about recent films showing in London. He had only been in Belgium two months, so he knew what was showing currently. I hadn't been on leave for a number of weeks so it could have been tricky, but I had seen "Gone with the Wind" and could describe Leicester Square, where I had seen the film, in some detail. I managed to convince him I was genuine, which, in the circumstances, was just as well for me.

I stayed in the bedroom of the Cafe for two days, watching the German troops passing by in the street below, and early on the third morning saw some Russian prisoners marched in from the surrounding district to the cinema next door. There they were paid for their labour in bread, black, tough, solid bread and as I was eating it too, I didn't think much to their wages. As a contrast to watching from the window, I tried to read some French history books belonging to Toon's father, but they were heavy going. I was wrestling with one of these, when Toon dashed in saying

"Get your clothes quickly, we have to move, the Gestapo are coming".

He went off into the other room overlooking the street and the front of the Cafe, whilst I collected coat, scarf and cap and tided up the bedroom. We went down the stairs, out of the back of the Cafe, through the garden and under a wire fence as fast as we could; this brought us to a path across a cornfield. As we walked slowly across this path trying to act naturally. Toon stopped me briefly and nodded towards two smartly dressed men who were walking on the road that led round to the front of the Cafe. "Gestapo", he whispered, I could only mutter that it was time for us to leave. We concealed ourselves on the far side of the cornfield for the rest of the afternoon, then he went back to see what had happened at his home.

'Coal Mine at Eisden' In theory Toon was employed here but used his access to dynamite for his sabotage activities

When he returned, he told me the full story. It appeared that the Gestapo had captured one of Toon's group (a woman) at a village nearby named Rechem. They knew that she did not have sufficient knowledge to be an informer, but she was a 'contact' who passed messages from one village to another. If she had been followed by the Gestapo, before her arrest, or if they had knowledge of her messages, the organisation would have problems, Toon in particular.

The warning about her arrest had come from a Resistance member employed in the local gendarmerie; some of the latter were very patriotic, others took the easy way out and handed any suspects over to the Germans (I expect they were paid for their treachery)

Toon decided that it would be safer for me to stay away from the Cafe, so we walked on to the house of a relation of his, who lived right on the Dutch border. It entailed crossing a canal, and as all the bridges were guarded and I had no identity papers, I was a bit worried. We crossed, however, by ferry which consisted of a wire stretched across the canal and a large flat-bottomed boat which was moved across by the simple method of the boatman pulling hand over hand on the wire. Toon paid for us both and I stood behind a German soldier breathing heavily down his neck, hoping I looked more like a Belgian than I felt.

When we reached Toon's relation she had no room to spare, not that she was aware of my identity. Toon did all the talking and I gathered that I was supposed to be a 'casual' Italian worker looking for a place to stay!

We returned a different way to the canal along the Belgian bank of the River Meuse. I looked across into Holland and thought about the battles those riverbanks had seen, including those of 1940, it wouldn't be long, I hoped, before they saw some liberating troops of ours. My troubles for that day were not over, for as we approached the canal we met a German patrol. This composed of three men, one officer and two other ranks fully equipped. The officer with machine gun slung from a cord around his neck and held across his chest, the two other ranks with rifles across their shoulders. The Officer wore his peaked hat, the soldiers their steel helmets and all three had hand grenades stuffed in their pockets and carried in a sling arrangement across their chests.

Toon told me later that their job was to make a patrol, looking for Belgian saboteurs, suspicious looking objects like myself, and generally keep an eye on the civilian population who might be up to nefarious acts of sabotage. They would stop and search anybody who they thought suspicious (and carried the weapons to deal with any trouble); they could check identity papers, which in my case were non existent, so we were in trouble if they stopped us.

Fortunately, the officer was telling the other two some joke and as we came abreast of them, they were all laughing and couldn't be bothered to stop the two Belgian civilians, one of whom was looking very pale indeed!

We re-crossed the canal by ferry, as before, and went to a large house nearby where a middle-aged woman answered our knock on the door. She invited us inside and Toon asked her directly whether she would mind looking after an English airman for that night. He didn't tell her that the subject under discussion was stood there and not saying much. "Oh no" said the woman "my husband has been taken by the Gestapo and is in prison, besides I have two children who would talk and if word got around that I sheltered an English airman we would all be shot".

1 think Toon was getting desperate by then, for he introduced me, and after much talking it was agreed that 1 could stay that night in the top room of the house, without the children knowing I was there. That was the first night of many that followed, where I hardly dared to breathe to avoid making a sound.

The next day Toon brought a cycle with him so we set off down the main road, but soon turned off to follow footpaths, which twisted and turned, sometimes rejoining the road for a while and quite often passing by German encampments in the woods. 1 thought it very suspicious for two cyclists to drift about along the footpaths, but as most of the locals used cycles we were not too conspicuous and nobody tried to stop us. We finished up at a small farm, where the farmer's wife proudly announced she had relatives in Canada, not that they could have helped her, if she was caught with me on the premises

After Toon had gone, she took me into a small sitting room and gave me a bowl of cherries whilst she went off to make a bed up for me. Suddenly there came a thunderous knocking on the door, and the woman ran back into the sitting room, moving very fast despite her mature years. She pointed for me to go into the bedroom, hissing "Deutsche" as she flashed past, which was enough for me. I shot off into the bedroom and. had the door closed before she had admitted the Germans. I couldn't hear what they were saying, it sounded to me like "where are the two men who have just cycled up?".

The only place to hide was under the bed, so I slid there and waited with my fingers crossed. It seemed a long time before they left, and the murmuring of voices went on and on, until finally the farmer's wife returned and I could crawl out from under the bed. 1 must have looked a picture, like an old witch with cobwebs dripping from my fingers and hair. She told me that the German soldiers had come to the farm asking for food, and she had had a hard job convincing them that she had no food, and was starving. I can understand their scepticism, for she was quite plump and provided me with two eggs and a large slice of bacon to prove how starved she was; we finished off the rest of the cherries, just in case!

Farmer's wife with husband and son (their cornfield was very draughty)

They may have gone away, but the German soldiers had a plot of their own. I had gone to bed about 10 P.M.., and was soon asleep but not for long, because the farmer's wife shook me awake. It seemed to me that she was holding my shoulder and the shaking was from her whole body, she was so frightened. Her husband had returned to find that the Germans had surrounded the house and it wasn't safe for me to stay in the house that night.

I agreed, but I had no idea where a safe place would be. I soon found out, for the farmer led me out of the house, round the back, and into a cornfield. The corn was about 2'6" - 3' high, so that when I ducked down I was out of sight, but it was very wet with dew and the night was cold. I had just got myself sorted out, 25 yards from the house, when the woman turned up and said I must go deeper into the cornfield, so I went in another 200 yards and tried to keep warm - a hopeless task.

Fortunately for me it did not rain during the night, but I was glad to see the dawn and even then it took until 10 A.M. for the morning to warm up. About 11 o'clock the farmer's wife came out, weaving through the corn, crouching down to avoid being seen, carrying a bottle of milk and some sandwiches. She said that the Germans had come that morning, early, to tell her that she must billet six N.C.O.'s on her farm; I don't think they believed her "starving" story, and were forcing the issue.

The farmhouse was not very big, and I could not see how she could billet 6 men, she did at least have a roofless pigsty adjoining the house, perhaps she put them in there.

Toon came for me at 1 o'clock following a message from the farmer's wife and we manoeuvred our way out of the cornfield to where he had hidden the cycles. We went back to his own home at the Cafe, had a meal, and cycled off back to the canal, where we crossed once more by ferry boat. Toon paid again! I still had no identity papers, but I was getting used to moving about, and having passed the first patrol safely, was under the illusion that I was safe enough without any. It was nearly a fatal mistake.

We called on Toon's sister, who lived in the small village of Stockkem. Toon was telling his sister the story that I was an Italian worker, and as I just sat and ate cherries, she never knew differently. She told us that a German patrol had searched every house in the street, looking for any evidence of Resistance activity, and above all checking Identity cards. Toon didn't seem to be concerned, so we left and cycled down a cobbled street, then on to the road that led out of the village.

As we passed the top of a side road, the German patrol, the usual officer and two fully armed men, were just about to turn into the same road as we were on. They were coming towards us, and although my German wasn't good, there was no misunderstanding what one of the men said to the officer, as he nodded towards us - "Shall we stop them?" "Oh no," the officer replied, it doesn't matter". I hope he got an Iron Cross before the end of the War, he deserved something for those few words.

When we got clear of the village we were both laughing, more with relief than anything. If Toon had been caught he would have been shot without much ceremony, and my position was not clear as I was masquerading in civilian clothes. (It was many years after the war that Toon confessed to me that he had a pistol under his coat and that he would have used it if they had stopped us. In view of his military activity with the International Brigade in Spain, his sabotage exploits and eventually his joint attack with the British Army later in 1944 I believed him!)

Dilsen

We came to a large farm at which I was supposed to stay the next 3 days, but it turned out to be 3 weeks. The aged farmer and his wife had two sons, Jeff and Theo, and a daughter, Anna. Jeff was a member of Toon's Resistance group; Theo did most of the farming, for apparently the farm was going to be his when the old man died. Anna was a qualified nurse, but was tied to the farm, looking after her parents and caring for her brothers. She was a real worker, and although she had some outside help that came in three days a week, she was always busy.

She greeted Toon and myself that afternoon, speaking Flemish, for the whole family, apart from Anna, spoke only Flemish, and she was quick to tell me not to try out my German on her father. For the old people's peace of mind they were told I was a Frenchman, hiding from the Germans, to avoid forced labour. The old father, particularly, would have thrown me out if he had suspected I was English, he was nervous for his family. He wasn't the only nervous one around; luckily he was not very perceptive; as a Frenchman I was not a great success, not many Frenchmen have difficulty conversing in their own language !

Whilst on the farm I kept to my own room most of the day; my identity was kept secret from outsiders, casual enquirers were told I was a visiting cousin. I played patience with an old pack of cards and for light reading had a French encyclopaedia A-K and L-Z. My meals were brought to me by Anna, and the rest of the family visited me from time to time, but as my Flemish was limited, conversation lagged and sign language took over. They didn't stay long!

A typical day was to wake about 8.30 A. M., wash, a few physical Jerks, not very enthusiastically, and by that time Anna would have arrived with a large amount of home made bread with butter and jam. After the meal, I would nip smartly across the farmyard to the "thunder box" which was alongside the pigsty. I tried not to draw breath too often, not only because of the pigs.

It took me only about 15 seconds to cross the yard each day, the only

The Farm at Dilsen (Photo taken in 1970)

opportunity that anybody passing could see me; yet at the end of 3 weeks, four people had seen me, and asked the family who I was.

During the morning I would play patience or read the encyclopaedia until lunch, which was usually a piece of salt bacon about an inch square, with a heap of potatoes and a mix-up of cabbage and beans. This put me to sleep for 2 to 3 hours, followed by some more cards or reading, a tea with bread and jam and an evening action packed, with perhaps a visit from one of the family. I would get to bed about 10 P.M. and sleep soundly until morning.

Time did not drag, however; I knew Toon was trying to get me moved on, and there were one or two incidents during my stay that kept me alert. The room I was in was quite small, with a window overlooking the garden, which was surrounded by walls and hedges so high that it was very secluded. Naturally, this garden was the pride and joy of the family, and their friends and relations were not averse to dropping in to be shown round, but not the lodger. I did manage to get out there long enough to pick the fruit, and help the family to eat it.

On the third morning of my stay, a company of German marines passed along the road outside, singing marching songs, rather like our troops singing "Roll out the Barrel". The difference was that the Germans were very good singers indeed, very melodious and in good marching time; I didn't object to them singing "Wir fahren gegen Engeland" (We march against England) if only they had stuck to singing instead of fighting.

Anna and the railway line to the mine (above)

Anna and the slag heap (Not a V1 site)

One evening, about a week later, I was carrying on a monologue with father - he was doing the talking - when Anna came in looking very pale and worried, she got rid of father without much ceremony. When he was out of earshot, she said "The Germans have come to the farm about 200 yards along the road, also the house of the Burgomeister (Mayor) and the house of the Doctor. They have thrown a cordon round each house and are even now searching the houses for hidden weapons. If they come here suspecting my brothers, they will find you".

I have read of people's knees knocking with fright and I now know how they felt, my stomach had no bottom to it and I literally shook for a few minutes, at the thought of having to dodge a cordon of armed soldiers. Luckily, Anna was so nervous she didn't notice and outwardly I must have looked calm.

We decided that there was no point in my making a break for it until they arrived, as I might blunder into them; with luck they would not come. Jeff and Theo came in, and apart from insisting that I should be ready to leave by the back window if the necessity arose, were very re-assuring that the Germans would not come. I think experience of German methods gave them an advantage, I wasn't so sure.

There was nobody more relieved than me, when I heard the cars of German soldiery and Gestapo leave the houses up the road and depart into the night about 11p.m. Although there was a risk they might return, I felt brave enough, now that they had gone, to go to bed, but I slept with my clothes handy, nevertheless! The search at the houses, so Anna said the next day, had found two old revolvers and an English flying helmet which the Germans had confiscated.(After the war, on a visit to the farm, I was told the true reason for the search, not looking for hidden weapons at all. An "informer" had put a notice on a tree in the middle of the village which read "There is an English airman hidden in the village".

The Germans had picked the wrong houses to search, and Anna had refrained from telling me the real object of their search).

Two days later Toon returned, although I had expected him sooner following the raiding party. He was more concerned for his Intelligence Officer 'Bob', the Wireless Operator, for he had suddenly disappeared and rumour had it that he had been shot at his set by the Gestapo.

Toon asked me whether I knew the Morse Code; it was arranged that if there were no further news of Bob, I would have a crack at sending messages back to England. I was glad to offer my help as something in return for all the help they were giving me, but I realised it would be a dangerous business - look what was supposed to have happened to Bob!

On the l6th July, Toon came in during the afternoon, and with much regret on the part of Anna and her brothers, I left the farm. I wasn't sorry to go, because I wanted to get on the path that led to Spain or Switzerland and beyond them, back home. As we cycled away, Toon told me he was sure everything would be fine, and that I would be home in 3 weeks, but I was sceptical and didn't allow myself to get too elated.

I was not aware that Toon's confidence in my return to England was due to the fact that our destination was a small general shop in Eisden about 3 miles away, run by Monsieur and Madame Janssen. She was part of the official escape route and had already passed several airmen like myself down the line. Toon must have been worried, however when Madame Janssen told us that her husband had been arrested.

The Gestapo had taken him for questioning because someone in the village had been firing off revolvers during the night. I suppose they expected the local store owner to know the likely tearaways in his district.

That put paid to my staying on the premises, but Madame Janssen had arranged for me to stay at another place in Eisden. (She spoke very good English and told me that she had been brought up in London and her brother still lived there)

The town was swarming with troops, and to avoid suspicion it was arranged that I would cycle part of the way with Toon, leave him, and then follow Madame Janssen who would be cycling ahead. She would lead on to the place where I was to stay, a jeweller's shop in the middle of town, dismount from her cycle and cough. I was to draw into the kerb, enter the shop and present an ear clip of Madame Janssen's, which the people there would recognise and look after me. That was the plan; like most plans, it went astray.

One benefit of being in official contact with the escape line was the false identity card I now carried, and supplied by Madame Janssen; it wasn't perfect, but it was better than nothing. Aircrew carried a set of head and shoulders photos whilst on operations, for just the purpose they were now used; the production of a false card, complete with photo.

1 felt more confident as I set off with Toon and passed another patrol; we crossed the ferry yet again, for the road across the bridge was guarded, and after bidding him goodbye, I followed Madame Janssen to the jewellers. So far, so good. I dismounted and waited whilst three soldiers

examined some watches in the window priced at 11,000 francs each, a lot more than they could afford I am sure, and eventually they moved away.

Eysden Ste Barbe (Limbourg). — Pauwengraaf

The Jewellers shop was in this street, right hand side No 24 opposite the brothel!

I stepped into the shop, which appeared deserted until a man came from behind a desk in the corner, where he had been repairing watches. I presented the ear-clip, and waited for the smile of recognition, but he merely looked at it and as I didn't say anything he asked me in French whether I wanted another one like it, turning to a tray full of ear-clips. Oh, I thought, he is stalling because there were some more German soldiers looking in the window, so I pretended to look at the tray of clips. After a while he said "I'm sorry, I haven't got one like that"; it was obvious he knew nothing of the plan so I tried the direct approach. "You don't understand" I said quietly "perhaps your wife knows". This baffled him completely, probably he didn't translate my anglicised French too easily, and we had reached deadlock, when fortunately Madame Janssen walked in to check that all was going to plan.

The shop owner knew her, of course, and left his idiot customer to shake her hand, a popular pastime in Belgium, still not connecting me with her at all. She rapidly explained the situation, however, and he called his wife who knew all about the plan and the ear-clip, but had not told her husband! I had arrived sooner than expected.

Madame Janssen (a courier and contact on the official Escape Line)

Mdme Janssen left us and I studied my helpers. The Jeweller Monsieur Duchene was aged about 50, small, with a neat moustache and nearly bald head, his manner was alert, he was an ex-serviceman of the 1914-18 war. He had earned the Croix de Guerre for escaping twice from the Germans, and was also a member of Toon's White Brigade, ready to fight again at the right moment, which wasn't far off. His wife, Madame Duchene was younger and taller than he, with jet back hair; dressed very smartly and wearing plenty of expensive looking jewellery. She helped in the shop, but was also a "guide" for allied airmen, taking them with her to Brussels or Antwerp. They had no children, which, I learned later, was a source

Monsieur Duchene, the jeweller (he had a rifle buried in his back garden and (below) Madame Duchene, his wife (both members of the official Escape Line)

79

of great regret to them; looking after "lost sheep", like myself, gave them pleasure, and a feeling of helping in their Country's struggle.

Behind the shop, which was quite small, was a sitting room where we had our meals, punctuated by the ring of the shop doorbell, which was operated by the opening of the outer shop door. The bell itself was situated in the sitting room and the first time I heard it I was on my feet in a flash, ready to go. It was that kind of strident bell that demands action! He was a very busy jeweller and the bell rang continuously; when I got too fed up with the noise I would go upstairs to the room that overlooked the street and watch the people passing below, standing well back from the net curtains. Directly opposite the jewellers was a cafe, and I was amazed at the number of German soldiers who came and went to this place. On querying this with the jeweller, he soon enlightened me - it was the local brothel!

One afternoon, a detachment of Hitler Youth went marching past, boys and girls marching with a very short pace. This gave them a military aspect, for it enabled the youngest of them, aged about 5 or 6 , to keep in step. There was something revolting' about them, their faces were deadly serious, they were singing as they marched about the "glorious Fatherland". At either side of the column slouched some youths, about 16 years old, dressed in brown Nazi uniforms, with the swastika on a brassard on their arms. They had revolvers slung from the waist, and looked like jailers marching beside their prisoners.

After I had been at the jewellers a few days, with periodic visits from Madame Janssen, I became accustomed to the soldiers entering the shop, and 1 used to go into the shop itself, talking with the jeweller until the soldiers came in. Their usual greeting was "Guten Tag" (Good day) so 1 would mutter 'Tag' and go over to the watch-repairing desk. There I would sit, with a watch in front of me, looking at it very knowingly with an eye lens, whilst the jeweller did the talking, and served the customers. The majority of these were soldiers, and always seemed to want the same thing, either a watch to be repaired, or to enquire the price of something in the window. On being told a price of anything over 200 Francs, they would find that they'd have to return tomorrow; it was a constant source of amusement. Often they would ask the jeweller if I was his son; his story was the same as that for his neighbours, I was his nephew, come to stay for a few weeks.

One thing I never get used to, was that the German soldiers would expect service at any time, and if the shop was closed they would come round to the back door, via a side alley and come in if the back gate had been left unlocked. We tried to remember to lock it at all times, but often at lunchtime with the shop shut, we listened to the news from London in English or French, and the noise of it would drown the knocking of a soldier on the back door.

Because that was locked, he would then knock on the window for attention; I think they thought they were a conquering army or something like that. Although 1 did not leave the house or back garden, 1 used to help by chopping wood for the fire outside the back door of the house. I was busy chopping away one morning, and I could sense somebody watching me. I glanced up at the back gate leading to the side alley and was confronted by a soldier in full uniform, plus rifle, slung from his shoulder. "Guten Tag" I said, hopefully, and to my relief he asked me if he could have his watch he'd left for repair.

The front shop door was closed, so he'd come round the back; by the look of all the equipment he was carrying he'd been posted to the Russian Front. With a quick nod, I dashed inside and called the jeweller's wife who came and attended to him, needless to say, 1 didn't chop any more wood near that gate.

My first visitor, apart from Madame Janssen, was Jacqueline, a young girl whose father and mother were at that time held prisoner by the Germans and they had been sentenced to death for aiding Allied airmen. She came to warn us that the Germans had two lorries in the town, in which they proposed to send Belgian civilians to Germany for forced labour (This was the day after the attempt on Hitler's life - July 21st - and Goebbels had announced that all available labour would be forced to work for Germany). To fill the lorry, the Germans had two systems.

The first was the one I had to fear most, which was to cordon off a block of buildings, then go through every house, taking all the men away for questioning after destroying all identity cards. Unless a man was a known collaborator of the Germans, all were transported as forced labour. The second method, and the one they used in this particular instance, was to surround a cinema and remove all the males after destroying identity cards. The point in destroying the cards was not only to create a excuse for arresting the men, but any men who were in an essential occupation and normally exempt from forced labour, lost their documents and became non-essential i.e. free to work for the Greater Reich.

There was one great advantage in hiding at a jeweller's shop, I had all his devices for protecting his shop from burglars, not that the Germans would have come like burglars, more like smash and grab! It was a help, though, that there was a bell in the jeweller's bedroom which rang when any one of four doors was opened, and all the windows were barred. Best of all was a skilfully concealed gap behind a brick wall in the cellar, built by the jeweller as a hiding place should the Germans be after him at any time, and available for me in an emergency.

The night that Jacqueline came to warn us of the round up, we waited up until 2 A.M., prepared to dive into the hiding place should they come through the houses, but all remained quiet. We discovered later that they had cleared out the cinema instead. Jacqueline's advance warning information came from her uncle, with whom she was staying; he was a prominent local citizen who was a collaborator with the Germans, but a patriot above all, supplying information to the Resistance.

Living among these brave people after four years of occupation one could see that apart from one's own family, there was only one way to survive; trust nobody, never give incriminating information to a stranger, or even a neighbour.

Madame Janssen called the following morning to confirm that the Germans had got their lorry loads and to tell us that someone had taken a shot at the local Mayor who was definitely a traitor. The Mayor had been cycling home for lunch and on being shot at, had the presence of mind to fall off his bike and fake being dead. The would be assassin/hero (depends which side you're on) had given up shooting for fear of hitting some children nearby.

She told us, also, that Jacqueline had heard that morning that her father had been shot and her mother sentenced to eight years imprisonment. The full story of her family was that they had fed and hidden several Allied airmen in their house at Brussels, but had been betrayed by a local neighbour. The Gestapo had taken the whole family. Father and Mother, Son and Daughter Jacqueline, for interrogation. Following this, the son had disappeared, probably into a forced labour gang, Father & Mother had been sentenced to death, and after a month of solitary confinement, Jacqueline had been sentenced to 11 months imprisonment. All this on hearsay from an informer, for the Gestapo had no proof, there were no Allied airmen in their home when they were arrested. If there had been flyers in the house, the family would have been shot immediately. To our helpers we were a walking death certificate.

Jacqueline had been out of prison a month when I had first met her and hoping that her parents' sentence of death would not be carried out;

they had been in prison a year. She called to see me that same evening, bringing her father's last letter, which he had written the day before he was shot. I had no easy answer for her grief, when she turned to me and said bitterly "He died for the English".

The next few days were quiet, except for odd moments of excitement as American Fortresses flew over; the daily help thought 1 stuttered due to my searching for the right word in French, but she was really none the wiser, being Polish and not understanding much French anyway. She too, had been told that I was the nephew, come to stay for a visit.

At the end of July, Madame Janssen suggested to the jeweller's wife that she hide two more evading airmen, and much against her will she agreed. 1 was pleased to think that I might meet some fellow travellers, although they obviously couldn't be more "nephews" visiting and would not have the comparative freedom that I enjoyed. It was decided that they would hide in a small room at the top of the house during the day, then come down in the evening when the shop was closed, and the daily help gone home.

The two airmen arrived the next day, led by Madame Janssen, they had come through Holland via the escape line. One was an American Navigator of a Flying Fortress, who had baled out over Holland, called "Chuck"; the other, named Albert, was an Air Bomber from a Lancaster. He had baled out over Germany, near Duisberg and walked into Holland before contacting the Resistance.

I was in the shop when they came in; they were very surprised when the jeweller's assistant stepped forward, held out his hand and said "Well, how goes it?" in English. Everything went well for about two days, until the daily help found the American wandering about upstairs. He seemed a particularly dim individual and had the idea that the whole organisation was being run for his benefit; making little effort to conceal himself, or even keep his loud American voice quiet. (He came from New York!) The jeweller and his wife rapidly became nervous and jumpy; the daily was warned that if she said anything she would be implicated, and as she herself was a Polish refugee, we were fairly safe.

The neighbours commented on the peculiar noises they could hear coming from the top room, (it was Chuck sneezing and talking) and the increased tension resulted in a near disaster. One lunchtime when the daily was on day off, the other two joined me in the sitting room behind the shop for a meal. I usually took it up to them, but as the maid was off, it was decided that they could come down for us all to eat together, with the shop door locked.

We were all settled around the table listening to the News in French, broadcast from London, with the volume turned up quite high, when there came a violent thumping on the door connecting the shop with our dining room. The jeweller had disconnected the circuit that rang the bell when the main shop door opened, but in his nervous and agitated state had forgotten to lock that same door. The noise of the radio had drowned the sounds of the impatient customers gathering in the shop, until one of them had got tired of waiting and thumped on our connecting door. When the jeweller opened the door six German soldiers stood there.

They were very cross: at having to wait for attention; luckily for us the noise of the radio had also drowned our English conversation. They must have heard the French news blaring out, but they said nothing and thought perhaps that it was one of their propaganda stations. The jeweller soon served them, and locked the door behind them.

After that episode, it would have been only a matter of time before one of us gave the game away completely, but the situation changed for two reasons. The first was that Madam Janssen's contacts on the escape line arranged for us to move on down to Liege as the next step of a journey to the Ardennes.

(We didn't know it at the time, but Airey Neave and M. I. 9 in London were trying to divert the evaders and escapers to a camp in the Ardennes, so that when the Allied army got near they could send a rescue column forward to the camp.) The story we were told, was that we were to join the Maquis Resistance fighters in the Ardennes eventually to liberate the area.

The second reason for the change in situation was that the local German Officer in charge of the Eisden district decided he wanted a Headquarters actually in the town itself, and picked on the jeweller's premises. He may have been aware of the attitude of the Jeweller, as an ex-soldier, to the Germans; he might even have had a suspicion of the jeweller's resistance activities, in any case he came in person to requisition the house.

The jeweller's wife spoke to him, as her husband was out, and I could hear them shouting at each other in the shop; it sounded such a quarrel that I had one hand on the door leading to the hideout. If they came into the back room to continue the argument I didn't propose to be around, but he left after delivering his ultimatum.

The jeweller and his wife had eight days to quit; the premises would be requisitioned. The reasons given were 1) the jeweller kept closed too long so that the Germans could not get their watches repaired, 2) he deliberately tampered with the watches so that they would not work for very long, and 3) the jeweller's wife was accused of jeering at German wounded as they passed through the town.

If they had searched the house they would have found 3 better reasons for requisitioning and a good excuse for eliminating the jeweller and his wife; the trumped up reasons given were pathetic.

The answers, that I am sure the Germans knew, were 1)The jeweller was swamped with work, mainly difficult repairs, which necessitated instruments and materials unobtainable during the war. He could not use petrol for cleaning and had to dismantle and brush each watch part; to get the repairs completed, he had to keep the shop closed during the early part of each morning. 2) He was too much of a craftsman to ruin a watch deliberately, even if it did belong to a German. 3) His wife was no different to most people, a wounded man had the sympathy of any onlooker and I doubt whether any of the women of Eisden jeered at wounded troops, certainly not Madame Duchene.

Madame Janssen was not keen on the move to Liege, but we had to go, the jeweller was going to appeal to a higher German officer, an Area Commander, but whatever the final decision we were on the move again.

Liege

Start of the journey to Liege

The two escape line men who had brought Albert and Chuck from Holland were controlled from London. They had forged ration cards, money, and had arranged the trip to Liege with their contacts. I was very sorry to leave the local patriots who had done so much for me at great risk to themselves, but I had to refuse Madame Janssen's offer to go to a farm across the border in Holland for the rest of the war.

I had also to refuse the offer from the jeweller and his wife, Monsieur and Madame Duchene, to stay with them wherever they had to go. Liege was one step nearer a route to home - so it was to Liege I had to go.

Due to a hitch in getting me another identity card, I left Eisden a day after the other two, the 10th August, my 22nd birthday. The method of transport was by tram, for the most part it resembled a narrow gauge railway, one engine and six coaches, which ran alongside the ordinary road. I had to change once, where the steam locomotives gave way to the more modern electric tramway nearer the big town of Liege.

The tram from Eisden departed at 5.30 A.M., so I was up at 4 for

86

breakfast and a tearful farewell from the jeweller's wife. I followed her husband at a discreet distance to the tram stop, which took about 15 minutes, I had been told that on boarding the tram I was to look for a boy and a woman, the latter would be wearing a baggy pair of slacks.

Sure enough, they were waiting on the platform of one of the coaches for me, but instead of ignoring me and keeping a distance as I thought they would, they clustered round the jeweller and myself and started a small discussion group. This worried me; it looked suspicious, the four of us herded on the platform of the tram, talking in whispers, when we could have sat inside the tram and talked naturally. It got worse; the boy disappeared to return with an Inspector of the tramway, who looked at me and said in a loud voice "Is this him?" and without waiting for a reply jumped off the platform waving for me to follow.

I gave the jeweller a quick handshake and hurried after the Inspector who took me to the guard's van. This was packed with tramway employees and as the journey progressed it became obvious that the Inspector's word was law, everybody treated him with deference. Taking me to one side he launched into the story of how he had helped over 300 airmen on to Liege, since the beginning of the War.

The conductor came collecting fares and turned away at a nod from the Inspector; I guess that all the employees of the tramway in that guard's van knew who I was, but they didn't speak to me. The patronage of the Inspector was useful, for when the time came to change from steam to electric, he told me to stay in the guard's van, whilst he stood at the door and diverted the electric tram alongside. We then passed smartly from one to the other before hordes of travellers crammed on.

It was very reminiscent of the London rush hour. The Inspector went off to check whether the Germans were inspecting passes or searching trams in Liege. He did this by cross-questioning the driver and conductor of the electric tram that had just come from Liege; when he was satisfied he gave the order for our tram to leave and we stood behind the driver for the next part of the journey.

The driver and Inspector chatted idly as we progressed. At each stop people poured on, unlike the London trams no attempt was made to keep people off the driver's platform, the whole tram soon became packed. The time was now about 8 A.M., and all the workers of Liege seemed to want to catch this tram, including several German soldiers complete with bulging kit bags.

The crush caused a problem for me with the conductor. He had seen me get on with the Inspector, but must have forgotten or had not been briefed, for in an excess of zeal, due, no doubt, to the Inspector's presence, he asked me whether I had a ticket, flicking his row of tickets suggestively as he did so. I had some money on me and could have asked for a ticket to Liege, but I knew that if I spoke, my accent would give me away. In addition, Liege was a large town and he might have asked me awkward questions about which part I wanted, and I hadn't a clue on that.

I just grinned at him and jerked my thumb towards the Inspector hoping that he would remember the connection. It worked, although whether he thought I was Gestapo or just another fare dodger I will never know, certainly he gave me a very dirty look as he vanished into the interior of the tram.

Proof of the Inspector's omnipotence came as we entered the outer suburb of Liege. The tram came to a halt at a small building in the middle of the road; a terminus for the trams consisting of a couple of rooms and a garage for a breakdown truck. As we drew up the Inspector said to the driver "Wait for me", jumped off the tram and entered the building. The morning sun was very warm by this time and the tram was packed full; the passengers soon began to fidget and pass rude remarks about the driver for delaying the departure. It started as muttered comments about the tramway and developed into harsh words and arm waving at the driver, they were just about to pull the tram apart when the Inspector returned.

He beckoned to me; so I pushed my way through the perspiring mob and joined him beside the tram, which departed at a lordly gesture from the Inspector. It seemed all very fishy to me; the passengers on the tram gazing out at the poor civilian who had been ordered off, so I just stared back at them as though I owned the tramway company.

The Inspector didn't seem worried, so I assumed I need not. He turned to me as the tram disappeared, saying that he was very sorry that I had been kept waiting; it seemed the other passengers didn't matter. He explained that the reason for the delay was that he had been 'phoning ahead to check on my destination.

We took the next tram and made a real tour round the city. We changed trams four or five times and at one stage of the journey we went straight through the middle of the town which was about the size of Coventry or Leicester. Liege straddles the River Meuse with about two-thirds of the city on the Western side, and the balance on the other side of the river. Public transport was limited to the tram service, which stopped running at dusk, the cobbled streets made cycling hazardous and there was a curfew after dark.

This particular day, however, the streets were crowded with people and the main square had a market with stalls set up in the middle. Our tram trundled through; most of the German soldiers on board descended from the tram as it stopped opposite a large building occupying all one side of the square. This was labelled with a banner reading KOMMANDANTUR, in black letters on a white background, stretching the whole face of the building. Add two sentries, a large swastika flag and some barbed wire - one certainly couldn't miss it.

We also changed trams in this Square and were joined by a very small German private lugging a hefty suitcase, which made the soldier in his uniform very hot indeed. This reminded the Inspector of a story he had heard from a friend of his in the Resistance.

It appeared that this friend was carrying a suitcase containing, among other things, some hand grenades. He was crossing one of the bridges that span the Meuse at Liege and was staggering somewhat under the weight of the case. Feeling a tap on his shoulder he turned to find a German soldier offering to carry the case (co-operate with civilians this week, deport them next), so they crossed the bridge together. At the other end was a German patrol which was stopping civilians and examining identity cards; "What have you got in the suitcase?" they enquired of the soldier. The Inspector's friend, who had been thinking how to explain the heavy weight, replied "Only some metal statues", and they were waved through. It sounded like a tall story to me, but there was no doubt that if the Belgians could score off the Germans in any way, it was their pleasure to do so.

We arrived eventually at the door of an Architect who had a constant stream of visitors; his doorbell rang incessantly but, as he told me, although it was very dangerous for so many people to come to his house, he wasn't perturbed - he had his "contacts". The significance of this statement was revealed later when I met some of his callers. I said goodbye to my Inspector friend, not expecting to see him again, and returned to my conversation with the Architect, interrupted yet again by the doorbell.

The civilian who entered was introduced, and started a lively discussion about arms and uniforms for the local White Brigade Resistance, and details of an expected parachute drop. They had just got going when another caller arrived who proved to be a young girl,

89

employed as a clerk in the German H. Q., that I had seen in the Square. She had information for the Resistance about an informer who had been denouncing patriots to the Gestapo. The girl clerk was attached to the Gestapo section that arrested the patriots, and her information was to be passed on by the Architect to another "liquidation" squad that dealt with informers.

That matter disposed of, the discussion on arms and uniforms resumed with the civilian; I tried to gather what his occupation was, and as he spoke it transpired that he was an actual member of the Gestapo. He was, on the surface, a person who the majority of Belgians hated most; a Belgian who had collaborated with the Germans and chosen to join the Gestapo. The Architect had a built-in insurance, if the local Gestapo became suspicious of his activities, he had a man on the inside to warn him.

I could not decide whether the Architect still practised, or got his income from London, or on the black market, but he kept a good table, for he laid on an excellent lunch of steak and chips followed by ice cream. Definitely my birthday!

During the afternoon a youth called to collect me, to rejoin Chuck and Albert who had come the same way as myself the previous day. The youth looked very tired and washed-out; he told me he had spent two days searching for arms dropped by parachute in the woods nearby. He had found them eventually, and buried them in the woods. He was very interested in the news that the girl clerk from the German H. Q. had given about the informer, who was a woman. He assured me that she wouldn't be around long, he had dealt with three such traitors personally.

I took the opportunity, after he left, to take a short nap - it had been an early start and I was due to move again. He returned about 6 o'clock with some friends who would accompany us. Nothing surprised me about the Architect's set up by this time, the "friends" comprised a Gendarme and another Gestapo man. I was given another good meal, and despite my protests that I was full, was assured that at our first stop to pick up a bicycle I would get yet another meal.

We set off, strolling along the streets, a rare bunch -a gendarme, two Gestapo men and an English airman. They did all the talking; I just tried to look nonchalant. I expect most of the passers-by thought that I was another poor devil who had been arrested and was being escorted to the lock-up! We walked for twenty minutes and arrived at the youth's home, where, as he had promised, I was given another meal, liver and chips this time with a glass of beer and a cup of coffee! Being too full for words, yet not wishing to appear discourteous in refusing all their hospitality, I started to eat, whilst all the neighbours came in to see the English airman, bringing with them photos of Englishmen they had known since 1914.

Somebody turned on the radio and tuned in to the News in English for my benefit (it happened to be a German station broadcasting in English) and they even went to fetch Grandpa out of his armchair to see me. Hospitality wasn't the word. I ate nearly half the meal, and had to give up, but thinking to encourage the conversation, which was buzzing along all round me, I idly mentioned that it was my birthday. That did it, all the females present had to kiss me at least three kisses each, an old Belgian custom, I was assured! I marvel that I survived.

At 8.30p.m. the youth and I left and cycled through the streets of Liege. He led me by about 200 yards, with a lot of fiddling around, including a couple of times when he waited for me to catch up, gave me instructions, then cycled off ahead. I thought that this was a dead give-away to any passer by who was observant. We came at last to a large house situated in a road that led to the river and the well-known bridges that the Americans had bombed and missed time after time, and the R. A. F. had missed all the other times.

The residents of the area were a mite sore about bombing, but the owner of the house was another member of the Underground organisation. His duties were to lead a band of men who stole food for the Maquis in the Ardennes, faked identity cards for all and sundry, collected guns and ammunition from parachute drops and eliminated traitors. All the members were armed; most had permits to carry them, as they doubled up as Gestapo men, in total they were a formidable combination.

I found Chuck and Albert installed in the house and the gang left us to it. Albert explained that the head of the gang was the Belgian Representative for Walt Disney, and was responsible for the distribution of cartoons and other animated films in Belgium. The Germans had stopped the release of these films, and he seemed to do little except trade shows of German films for German officers, in a small cinema that was attached to the house. I could imagine what those films were about!

The house owner was tall, well dressed, but heavily built and as we didn't know his name, nor wanted to, we nicknamed him 'Fatty'. He had all the trappings of a successful businessman, a large house in a fashionable part of town, apparent wealth and a very chic wife.

The other members of the gang were supposedly artists and animators in his firm; they became animated at night when they stole food and went looking for supply drops. Fatty didn't sleep in this house, but used it as a work place, upstairs he kept a very large bed should he wish to stay over night. The bed was so large that the three of us. Chuck Albert and myself were to sleep in it; unfortunately I lost the toss and went in the middle. In Winter that would have been fine, but in mid-summer 1944 it was far too hot.

We took our shoes off to avoid any noise, and started a tour of inspection, put all the lights out, except one, which was reflected in a large mirror against the wall. Albert hadn't noticed the mirror and as we were creeping across the room he flattened out suddenly on the floor We were so used to doing things and thinking afterwards ("twitchy" was the word used to describe us) that Chuck and I threw ourselves down as well. "I saw something moving behind the light" said Albert; upon investigation it proved to be his own reflection in the mirror!

We went to bed after that scare and very warm it was, squashed three in a bed, until Chuck got up early in the morning and I was able to cool off. I vowed 1 would sleep on the floor the next night; as it turned out this wasn't necessary. A maid, named Marie, turned up during the morning; she was really something special, with blonde hair and a peaches and cream complexion, I expect 'Fatty' had promised her a part in films after the War!

He arrived, to show us a back exit, in case the house was raided; I am glad we did not have to use it, as it entailed crossing two back gardens and through another house in the next street. The snag was that German officers were billeted in the houses with the back gardens; the occupants of the house we had to pass through were in ignorance of the whole arrangement. In an emergency we wouldn't have time to explain to them why we were just passing through.

Fatty had decided that, in any event, we were too much of a risk to have around his house, so he got working on our false identity cards and fitted us up with cards for Liege. I became Jean Artur Briard, it showed that I worked on the Belgian railways (Reserved occupation) and my work permit was stamped with the official German stamp every six months from April 1943 to date. Very efficient.

He arranged that another courier would take us to a farm on the outskirts of the town and that afternoon we met "Willie". He looked about 30, but his real age was only 18; he had dyed his hair, and wore spectacles with plain glass lens. The ageing wrinkles on his face, however, were genuine;

they came from sabotage and fighting in the Ardennes. The Germans had recruited Russian traitors to fight the Belgian guerrillas in the Ardennes, whilst they got on with the real war.

Willie decided that for the move to the farm, I should go ahead with another member of the gang, and he would follow with Chuck and Albert, our rendezvous a cafe in the Northern side of the town, near the farm. The risky part of the journey was that we had to pass three bridges, at the ends of which, during the previous days, the Germans had been collecting all the young men and putting them in lorries for transport to Germany as. forced labour. It was a dangerous habit of theirs. On this particular day, all such activity had ceased, so it was decided to move us.

Liege (northern suburb)

I left, as arranged, with another man and we walked along the road beside the river, past the bridges and finally caught a No. 5 tram which took us to the outskirts. Before long, the others arrived at our cafe rendezvous; we had made it, without incident The three of us expected that we would be well fed and comfortable at the farm, but we were mistaken. All the previous places where I had been hidden, including the farm near Eisden, were like palaces compared with this farm.

The whole place was filthy; the kitchen was filled with a swarm of flies, the most I have ever seen in one room. We arrived in the evening and had a meal, consisting of bread and treacle (good stuff for flies) and hot milk, with flies trying to drown themselves; We met the farmer's family, his wife and one daughter; both these ladies were over-weight, which surprised us considering it was wartime; we found the reason later.   We also met the farmer's four sons, aged from about 30 to the youngest about 9.

After we had eaten, we were taken out to the barn and shown an enormous pile of straw in which we were to sleep, plus a special back exit. Sleep we did, despite the ticks and other insects in the straw, which tried to make life interesting for us.

The following days were more pleasant, for the farm had two large orchards away from the farmhouse and we spent most of the days eating pears and apples and sunbathing. Chuck couldn't get it into his head that a low profile was vital, and was rude to all and sundry. Albert and I were dragged in as interpreters and soon got fed up, avoiding him as much as possible. The farmer's young sons ragged and teased him and he didn't help himself by losing his temper with them, chasing them round the farmyard.

We saw little of our guide, Willie, for he was very occupied with the gang in Liege and rarely visited us. He told us that he was kept busy stealing food, but he promised that we would move on as soon as arrangements could be made. The food we were given on the farm was

94

very poor, in fact for a farm it was surprisingly poor, but was due to the farmer selling his stock and produce on the Black Market.

He slaughtered four pigs whilst we were there, as he told us "to prevent them going to the Germans" but the people who lived around the farm told us what really went on. He made tremendous profits selling to the Black Market, and from the size of his wife and daughter not all of the pork was sold off, certainly we didn't get any.

In the orchards were two men, employed by the farmer as watchers, night and day, to protect his fruit from being stolen. They were useful to us in keeping an eye open for German troops, although there were none in the immediate vicinity of the farm.

We used to talk about the War with them, and were often joined by an old man who lived locally. He had been an officer in the First World War and was known in the district to all and sundry as the "Adjutant". He came to the farm to buy the produce, and he confirmed that the farmer was indeed running a good racket with the Black Market.

The Adjutant had the only wireless set in the area, and was our only source of news. The Allied Forces had managed to break out of Normandy, and it was the time of the "Falaise Gap" when the German troops were trapped in the Falaise pocket and being shot up by the fighter bombers. We were glad to hear of the progress towards us, however far away it seemed.

We hoped to see the R. A. F. fighters or medium bombers any day, but it wasn't the R. A. F. who arrived, it was the American Fortresses. It was 2.30 in the afternoon, Albert and I were asleep in the orchard; I was dreaming about aeroplanes, and it was all part of the dream, when there was a sound of sirens, followed by the drone of aircraft. Dreams became reality when a flack battery let rip and the noise of aircraft came from immediately overhead. They had approached from the sun, and we could not see them until they had bombed and were turning for home. The flack was noisy, but not intensive and very inaccurate Not surprising, for the aircraft were at least 15,000ft; and when they released their bombs the American method of bombing became clear. Their lead aircraft gave the signal for them to release their bombs all together, which from the ground resulted in one combined "swish" as the bombs arrived, the explosions following were like somebody beating a tattoo on a drum.

The bombs seemed to have dropped some distance away, so we were not unduly alarmed until fragments of flack began to "ping" down into the orchard, cutting through the leaves, and thudding into the soft earth.

We nipped smartly under a thick bough and stopped being brave Englishmen gazing up at their American Allies knocking hell out of the Germans. That's how it should have been; unfortunately, the Forts had missed their objective (one of the bridges) and killed a large number of civilians. We only heard about that, however, some time later.

Willie had not contacted us for three days, the longest period yet; we were beginning to think that the Germans had caught him. The farmer was not a member of the organisation and could not give us any information on his whereabouts; we were anxious to see Willie and get on our way.

He arrived at just the right time to sort out a problem that Chuck had got us into. Two strangers, Gendarmes, had come into the Orchard and were talking to one of the fruit pickers. Chuck had walked up to them, picked up one of the Gendarmes capes, borrowed one of their hats, by sign language, and dressed up as a Gendarme. He then broke into a conversation in English! Willie quickly explained who we were, and luckily they were sympathetic and wished us luck, but as they pointed out, and as everybody realised, except Chuck, they could have been the wrong type of Gendarme, (pro-German), and that would have been disaster for all of us.

The Adjutant asked me whether I would go back into Liege with him to see his old mother, who was bedridden. He said she would like to meet an Englishman again, our soldiers of the 1914/18 War must have left many memories in Belgium. I felt I needed some exercise, and he assured me that we could avoid walking where there were German patrols. I went with him and his daughter to the tram terminus, which was close to the farm and as we waited I said jokingly "If my Inspector is on this tram he'd get a shock".

We got the shock, however, for he was on the tram, and on seeing me he took the Adjutant to one side and did his celebrated "hold the tram" act. After an animated conversation, we all got on the tram and went off - one stop - then we all got off again The Inspector explained that the Germans were inspecting identity cards on the trams, and it was not advisable for us to go into Liege, it was extremely fortunate that we had met him.

He told me, also, that the Architect had left Liege in a hurry. He had been tipped off that the German Gestapo were after him (no doubt by his Belgian Gestapo friends). The Inspector was now in contact with the head of the organisation in Liege, and he would take me directly to him. I didn't want to leave Albert at the farm so abruptly, so I fixed to go back, collect Albert and meet the Inspector for a tram that left about 1.25p.m. According to the Inspector, the Germans would be on their lunch break at this time; the identity card inspection job was very boring for the soldiers, and they conducted it as far as possible from the nearest bar. I thought that a little British.

That finished my trip to see the Adjutant's Mother, but we went for a walk before returning to the farm, where I told Albert we were going to move. He wasn't at all enthusiastic; he was fed up and didn't expect much help from the "head of the organisation" in Liege. He reasoned that we had seen too many "heads" already, but the alternative for him was to stay on the farm with the flies and the straw, so reluctantly he joined me and we left together to catch the tram.

Before we left, Willie phoned the farm to say that he too had fixed for us to leave the following day, but we decided to go while we could, waiting a day could alter the whole outcome in that set-up. We left Chuck to follow with Willie the next day, and as it turned out, Willie was in contact with the same man as the Inspector, so Chuck was brought to the same destination as ourselves.

The Inspector met Albert and myself on the tram and we went down to Liege; he was checking that the Germans were not on the trams by quizzing the conductors on the "out" line as we went in. Once more we went all round the town by tram, and then walked around the streets for a time because there was nobody at the rendezvous. We were due to meet up with "George", the current head of the organisation, and eventually he arrived and we looked forward to getting on our way home again.

We said goodbye to the Inspector, with many thanks, and went to a private house, where we stayed for two days, visited occasionally by George and another man. The two of them seemed very active in the underground movement, and I heard, subsequent to the liberation of Liege, that they had been involved in street battles with the Germans, one of the two being killed.

We were well cared for, our host and his family did their best to entertain us, but we were glad to be on the move again, with a lady and a young girl, aged 17, who took us to the outer suburbs of Liege, then across the Meuse by tram. They took particular note to cross the one bridge that the Germans were not patrolling; although they told us that random checks on pedestrians were often carried out. The Liege bridges in 1944 were no place for anyone with a nervous disposition; if you were not being stopped and questioned by the German soldiery, you were

97

bombed by the Fortresses and R. A. F.

As we progressed, the lady explained that they had other ways of getting airmen across the bridge, which they had used on previous occasions. One, they had used, was in co-operation with the Gendarmerie (the good ones) where they had "borrowed" one of their Black Marias, or Belgian equivalent, loaded it up with airmen, and driven across the bridge with their "prisoners".

When we arrived at our destination, a house in the small town of Seraing, in the South West suburbs of Liege, I was separated from Albert, who went to the girl's house and I went to the lady's home. Here I met her husband, and their other "lodger", a young Frenchman waiting to go to the Ardennes to fight with the Maquis.

The couple were in their fifties, their name Grandet and their son had been a prisoner of war since 1940. They had carried on the fight by helping every kind of Allied serviceman they could. When I arrived, they had six Russians, ten Americans, four British and a Frenchman, hidden in the district. They personally visited each one of them at least every two days, and had already passed innumerable men along the line to the South. Now, however, the line was cut and when I arrived, a good concentration of human dynamite was being collected.

Over lunch, they told me that it would be better if I didn't get any ideas about striking out on my own; not that I had any. Two high ranking American officers they had sheltered had done just that and were picked up by the Gestapo within 24 hours.

The Frenchman had an interesting story, he came from Brest, and in 1942 had been participating in some useful sabotage. He had been arrested by the Germans for a job that he hadn't done, fortunately for him, and as they could find no proof they sentenced him to two years in a German prison, just for luck. He was in prison near the oil plant at Wesseling, our target for the night of June 21st, the one we personally did not reach; moreover he was working in the plant that night (forced labour).The attack had not been a success, he said, the bombs had been well clear of the plant.

The amazing part of his story to me, however, was that when he was released from prison, he was given a ticket to Paris and set free at the prison gate in Germany. They let him go, knowing or suspecting he was a saboteur, in the heart of the Ruhr. He went to Aachen, where he had friends, spent a lively couple of weeks with some sabotage, moved on to Monsieur Grandet in Liege, and was going down to the Ardennes to carry on the fight and sabotage with the Maquis.

Later that afternoon I was introduced to the local Priest, who was placing all these dangerous evaders among his parishioners. He had to know and trust his flock, for if just one of them betrayed him to the Germans, half the parish would have been shot. He was a Roman Catholic priest, but that did not stop him helping all Allied men, whatever their religion, he was a good example of what Christianity should be.

Three evaders in hiding with M Grandet. Me, a Russian and a Frenchman

Seraing (southern suburb of Liege)

The family he selected to look after me, consisted of an elderly couple, Monsieur and Madame Schmidt, who had three children, Paul, Marie and Elizabeth. Paul had his own house nearby, Elizabeth was single and lived at home with the elderly parents, and Marie, who was married, lived in a house that was behind her parent's home. Marie's husband, Rene Haccart was a watchman at one of the local factories, and the family decided between them that I should stay with Marie and Rene.

House in Seraing with Marie, Elizabeth, their mother and Marie Therese

Marie, Rene and Marie Therese

Their three-storied house was built on the side of a hill and was very narrow, just one room in width. It was completely detached and the back garden sloped down to the cottage where Elizabeth lived with the elderly couple. It was dark when I arrived, so I didn't appreciate the position of the house until Rene took me up to the bedroom at the top of the house overlooking the valley.

Even though it was dark, the view was magnificent; one could see the whole width of the valley stretched out below and here and there the odd glimmer of light. This puzzled me, for black out regulations in Occupied Europe were strictly enforced, as Rene opened the window and the cool night breeze flowed in, I could hear the noise of machinery operating. I realised, thinking of Rene's job as watchman, that I was looking down on a factory complex, at work night and day, and I asked Rene what the factories were doing. His answer wasn't re-assuring, they were synthetic oil plants, munition and engineering factories spread out along the riverbank only half a mile away.

In daylight, the next morning, I had a good look at them spread out below me, they were a very tempting target. They had been attacked, successfully, the previous year by R. A. F. Mosquitos flying in at low level, and the local citizens were well pleased with the R. A. F. The American Fortresses had also bombed from 15,000' and had caused more damage to civilian houses than the factories. I don't suppose that the R. A. F. would have been any more accurate from 15,000', but if either Air Force decided to return, the half a mile from me to the target wasn't far enough!

For two days all was quiet, Rene's Mother had just died and he and his wife Marie were busy with the preparations for the funeral. I was kept busy, however, amusing their only daughter, Marie Therese, aged five, who was told that I was a cousin come to visit them. Luckily she wasn't old enough to notice my halting French, and she was bluffed completely (at least I kidded someone) as was proved later, for she told the neighbours, who had seen me in the garden, that I was her cousin.

Meanwhile, the factories worked on 24 hours round the clock.

It was about 6 o'clock on the afternoon of the funeral of Rene's Mother, and the family had returned to Rene's house for a meal. We were seated at the table, Rene and Marie, her sister Elizabeth and Rene's Father, who did not say much, which wasn't surprising as he had just buried his wife. The elderly parents in the cottage below were looking after Marie Therese, who was playing there with a friend. The air-raid siren had sounded some 15 minutes earlier. Planes had been passing over (as they often did) and some optimist had sounded the All Clear.

The background drone of the planes became very loud, and a flak battery in the valley opened up. Rene was nervous about aircraft, he had been on duty when the Mosquitos attacked his factory; he was justifiably twitchy.

The proximity of the factories had not helped my nerves either, and when, coupled with the crack of guns, I heard a familiar swishing sound, I dived for the underside of the stairs in next to no time. Rene beat me to it, only because he was nearer! The old man sat impassively in his chair, and as the explosions of the bombs set the house dancing, Marie and Elizabeth calmly walked round opening the doors and windows. This may have been the local Air Raid Precautions, or perhaps they thought they could hear the noise better. I felt rather foolish, crouched under the stairs, hands behind my head and mouth open for blast, whilst they walked around opening windows.

It took a second wave of bombs and a third load to make them utter a sound, and join us under the stairs, where at least we had a brick wall on one side. Unfortunately, the Fortresses had not been very accurate, they had aimed at three synthetic oil plants; one they had hit fair and square and it was burning well, but the other two units they had missed completely, all their bombs falling on small civilian houses, bracketing the house I was in.

They were only 500lb bombs, but they killed many Belgians. The first two groups of aircraft had undershot their target by 1000 yards, only the third group had been effective; I didn't enjoy my position as ground observer. To be killed in an Allied air raid after having survived so far would have been ironic to say the least.

We resumed our meal, but before long we had a visitor, a neighbour of Rene's father, to tell us that the latter's house had been demolished in the bombing. The whole family had been in that house earlier in the afternoon, following the funeral, and they all began congratulating themselves on their lucky escape. All except Rene's father, who just sat quietly, I don't think he would have minded being in his own house during the bombing.

From experience, I knew that if one Air Force did not hit the target, round the clock bombing meant that the R. A. F. would probably be over the following night, so I had all my clothes ready for a quick dive for shelter. Two nights later, as I went up to bed, about 10.30p.m., there was a thick ground mist in the valley so I was not expecting any trouble. An hour later, however, the sirens wailed and a single plane flew over dropping a marker flare over the factory as it went   I waited with some trepidation for the rest of the force to arrive, but nothing further happened. I could only assume that it was a decoy and the attack went somewhere else.

Liberation

It was now the beginning of September 1944 and the battlefront was moving rapidly up to the Belgian border. During daylight I could look across and see Spitfires and Lightning fighters heading for targets on the main road on the opposite side of the valley. I could see them diving and twisting then levelling out, followed by the noise of their dive and rattle of guns, the thumps of their bombs echoing across the valley. The fighters were not aware of the flak battery, positioned by the oil plant in the bottom of the valley, and it was frustrating to watch them fly into range of the guns, straight and level. As the flak burst around them, they had to jink and weave all over the sky to escape, and although I saw no direct hits, there were some who had to tie themselves in knots to get away from it.

Monsiuer and Madame Grandet with some of the evaders, September 1944 (There are 4 Russians in the group, they escaped from working parties

Parish Priest and helper with evaders September 1944

The continuous stream of these aircraft over the town got the flak gunners trigger happy, for they fired at anything within range, including one of their own light spotter planes, which flew low over the house at about 100ft with flak bursting all round it. I didn't mind that, but the flak splinters showered down like rain and the crack of the shells exploding so close was like bomb bursts.

The echoes accentuated the noise across the valley and I thought it prudent to go to the air raid shelter in the garden. When things quietened down, I emerged to find Monsieur and Madame Grandet waiting in the empty house, they had been caught in the open, and had to rush for the house, only to find it deserted.

Liberation was at hand they felt, and they had decided to have a celebration in their house with all the evaders in the neighbourhood, twelve all told; they had come to invite me for that evening.

I went down alone and met the rest of them; Americans, Russians and British including my friend Albert, who I had been visiting after dark in the company of Monsieur Grandet. The party went with a swing, we had plenty to celebrate and cognac to do it with. We expected the American troops to arrive the following day, as they were rumoured to be at Namur and that day, the 3rd September, the British had entered Brussels, we were in good spirits, even before we started on the brandy.

A few of the people who had helped us arrived to join the party, including Marie, my own helper. Monsieur Grandet's brother gave a short speech saying how glad they had been to help us and how much it meant to them to be able to serve their country in this way. The answer to this speech fell to my lot, and it was an advantage to me that I had had some brandy to loosen my tongue. I apologised for my anglicised French, but I tried to tell them how grateful we all were and stressed the fact that we all realised that they had risked their very lives for us, which made us eternally grateful. All very difficult to put into coherent French, but they got the gist and it seemed to go down very well.

Albert came back with me after the party, and stayed overnight. I showed him the view from my window, which shook him somewhat, he had not realised how close we all were to the factories and oil plants, "Roll on the Americans and liberation" he said.

By now, one could hear artillery batteries firing in the surrounding hills, the noise like thunder; at night, flashes lit the sky from the direction of Namur. A battle was going on in the Ardennes forest, which flanked the main road leading to Seraing and Liege. Fighter activity increased and they attacked a flak battery, which was on top of a plateau on the other side of the valley. The battery in the bottom of the valley they left alone, probably because it was sited near the oil plant The battery they did attack, started using it's guns as ordinary artillery, opening fire across the valley at some unseen target behind the house I was in, and out of my view. The whistle of the shell passing the house on its way across the valley was eerie, and I was anticipating some counter fire from my side. When the reply came, however, it was from very close range to the battery, and from my observation post at the window I could see the shells bursting on the gun position.

German guns behind me banged off occasionally and this went on for two hours until the advancing Americans appeared to be closing in on the battery. The German gunners in the bottom of the valley opened up on them with tracer shells, very spectacular, but several houses caught fire as the tracer got amongst them. There seemed to be no answering fire from the Americans, but they must have pressed on because the battery on the knoll suddenly blew up, followed by a succession of explosions as the bridges over the Meuse were blown; it seemed the Germans were pulling out.

They had been filing past on the main road back to the border for some days, reports from onlookers said that they looked a sorry lot and they were commandeering anything that could carry them. Albert had a narrow shave for he was in the garage of the house where he was in hiding (a baker's shop) when three German soldiers came in and told him they were taking the Baker's van. Albert did not stop to argue, and rushed off to tell the baker who was dismayed and annoyed to see his van go, but relieved that they hadn't realised who Albert was.

Apart from odd shots, firing stopped around 6 o'clock and later that evening came the sound of cheering from a carload of Belgian youths. They were touring round, telling everybody to put their flags out, for the Americans were coming; this was about 7 o'clock. At 8 o'clock they were back again, saying "take the flags in", because some Germans were still around and shooting at the houses with flags, in a spirit of revenge. Confusion all round!

The following morning I borrowed a suit from Rene, and despite his shoes pinching a bit, I strolled along the main street of Seraing awaiting the American Army, along with a group of evaders.

They came, first a jeep containing an American Colonel with driver and a .5 machine gun mounted on the bonnet. Everybody cheered and shouted Vive L'Amerique as they went past, and one of the American evaders in our group bellowed "Get a move on Joe", which made the Colonel turn and stare.

Troops in trucks followed on, and all that day the Americans were moving up; I spoke to several of them, much to their surprise, for they expected a flow of French. One told me that I spoke very good English, and he was obviously pleased to find someone he could talk to.

Now the Liberation had arrived, Rene and his wife could tell the neighbours all about their "visitor" and I had an afternoon of cross-questioning about England, food and rationing, the R. A. F., and how I got to Seraing. I was aware that it would not be wise to say who had helped me get thus far, so I just told them I had dropped in by parachute a few miles to the North. They had all believed Marie Therese when she told them I was her cousin.

That evening a special Thanksgiving Service was planned in the local Roman Catholic Church, conducted, of course, by the Priest who had played such a big part in helping us.

The highlight was to be a grand entry into the Church of all the evaders in the district, so that the parishioners could see what their Priest and fellow parishioners had been looking after, unknown to the majority. At 6 o'clock, therefore, Rene, Marie and myself went to a Cafe near the

Church where the evaders were to assemble prior to the service. We were besieged for our autograph (fame at last!), and at a blast from the whistle of a Boy Scout leader, we all formed up, three abreast, with a line of Boy Scouts each side, and we marched off to the Church.

Our entry was grand indeed, a kind of slow march; it had to be slow, for I was supporting the American next to me who had been celebrating all day. I suggested to him that during the service he should watch me and do the same as myself. This would have been fine, but he had reached the happy state of not being able to see much at all.

The service was a long sequence of standing and kneeling, made difficult for us because we were all in the front and could not see what the rest of the congregation were doing. It didn't matter too much to my American friend, he swayed like a tree in a gale when he stood up, and leaned against me until I lowered him down again. Towards the end of the service I became aware of whispering and banging about behind in the pews, and when we came to leave, half the congregation had vanished, our dignified exit became a bit rushed.

The rumour had come, during the service, that the Germans were returning and most people decided it would be wiser to leave, than hear the sermon. For the evaders and their helpers, if the rumour was true, we were in trouble, the whole district knew who we were, and where we were staying!

The Germans did, in fact, return the next day, via the Luftwaffe; several aircraft decided to strafe the town of Seraing, and the hill on which I was staying. I was getting a long delayed haircut in a hairdressers at the foot of the hill, and had to take shelter in the basement. The planes attacked with bombs and cannon fire diving down over the hill, I expect they could see the American troops on the valley road, but their bombs and cannon shells only whistled and banged among the houses on the hill. When I returned to Marie's, after they had gone, a bomb had fallen only yards from her house on a deserted property, but shrapnel had broken Marie's front window and I found a bomb splinter under the bed, still warm. (Not always the safest place!)

Two civilians were killed in another house nearby, they had narrowly missed death during the American attacks earlier, but otherwise the cannon fire had caused only a few holes and a lot of dud shells A small boy proudly presented me with one of the unexploded cannon shells, as a souvenir. After thanking him for his gift, I dumped it in a safe place as soon as I could - the bottom of a large emergency water supply tank.

Albert and I went out that evening and joined the other evaders for a drink to celebrate our departure the following day to get back to England. Several of the Belgian helpers joined in, and the party soon went into top gear; events became hazy, and I remember going from one bar to another. In one, we were dancing with half the population of Seraing, and the other half were watching from the doorway and pressed against the windows. I was wearing a heavy pair of boots but couldn't feel them at all; I feel sorry for the girls I was dancing with.

Somebody took me home at the end of the evening and I can remember the look of surprise on Rene's face when the door opened, I only have his word that I spoke fluent French to him, whilst he put me to bed. I wasn't feeling too good the next morning and as I awoke I went over to the window for some fresh air, just in time to see a bomb burst in the valley below. The noise of the explosion coincided with the roar of the aircraft's engines as it scooted off. I was dressed and down the stairs in a flash, in time to hear the air raid siren sound the warning. Just not organised.

The siren sounding had degenerated into a shambles, they gave a warning for any aeroplane that came near, friend or foe, sometimes the warning and all clear sounded all in one long wail. The front line of the War was here.

Monsieur Grandet agreed to accompany all the evaders in his care into Liege that afternoon, to seek out the American Officer who was appointed to control the town We, that is the Americans and British, were anxious to return to England, Monsieur Grandet was concerned also for the Russian evaders whom we would have to leave behind in Seraing.

After a fond farewell to Marie, Rene and the family, I joined the others and we made our way into Liege. The aircraft that had bombed that morning decided to have another try. It was a Messerschmitt 110 diving out of the sun, with it's engines throttled hack, aiming at the pontoon bridge that the Americans had thrown across the river. Unlike the morning attack, the American A. A. gunners had seen it coming, and opened up with about thirty .5 machine guns. The noise was sudden and startling and the plane was hit, for it disappeared, trailing smoke, over the nearby hills.

In Liege itself there was chaos; American trucks were going in all directions, and at the office of the Town Major, as he was called, a very harassed officer was trying to cope with all sorts of problems. To him, evaders were a pain in the neck; he had been meeting several a day since he had left his base in Paris, if we could wait a week something could be organised.

We were not going to hang around for another week, we could make our own decisions now, so if Paris was the base, we must get there by hitch-hiking, with luck, we might find an airfield on the way.

We said goodbye to Monsieur Grandet, still trying to get the Americans to do something for his Russians, and went down to the pontoon bridge. Streams of traffic were going in both directions, but nothing was travelling as far as Paris that evening as it was getting late, around 5 P.M.. We did, however, hitch a ride to a point about 5 miles outside the town where an American A. A. battery was stationed. The troops there told us that they had a truck going through to Paris the next day and gave us some of their 'K' rations - chopped meat (Spam), sweets, biscuits and chocolate.

Our party consisted of 8 Americans, 2 Englishmen, 1 Australian and 1 New Zealander, and we bedded down, with a couple of blankets each, in a house which the Gunners had requisitioned, alongside the gun site. My sleep was not peaceful; we were trying to sleep on a parquet floor, and the gun battery let rip at night raiders every few minutes, but we were progressing.

The truck they were expecting, did not arrive the next morning, but they received instructions from their H. Q. to take us to a collection centre, from where we would be flown home. Wonderful, we all thought, what an organised lot these Americans are - of course we should have known that it wouldn't be that easy. A truck took us to the collection centre, which turned out to be a camp for captured German prisoners, where they were sorted out and despatched back to Paris by truck.

We reverted to plan one, and rode shotgun on the P. O. W. trucks and on that first day got as far as a P. O. W. cage at Lille. The M. P. 's guarding the prisoners made us welcome, and shared their rations and their hayloft with us. To help us on our way the next day, they detailed two soldiers and a special lorry to take us to the main Brussels to Paris road where there was plenty of traffic. To reach this road we passed through several villages and as we were still in civilian clothes we got some very black looks from the locals. As we halted momentarily at a crossroads, I overheard one woman say to her friend "Look, they are arresting the collaborators already".

We didn't have to wait long, for our lift to Paris as yet 200 miles away; once we had reached the main road; we climbed aboard, feeling that we were on the last stage of our journey.

Paris

We arrived at the outskirts of Paris at about 10p.m. and left the truck at a road junction, where stood an American military policeman. (Better known as a 'Snowdrop')

His response to our enquiry for his H. Q. was startling; he brandished his rifle and backed away mumbling in some language, which wasn't French or English. We couldn't get any sense out of him; he seemed to think we were French civilians come to beat him up; he'd had a few drinks and even the Americans among us couldn't get through to him.

We flagged down a jeep driven by a U. S. 9th Air Force officer, explained who we were, and he took us to his H.Q. which was due to move out the next day to Liege of all places. There were few personnel left there, and nobody had a clue on what to do with evaders; but there were plenty of beds. Our civilian clothes brought a comment from one American officer "Geez, bloody scroungers moving in before we're even gone". His face was a picture when one of his compatriots in our group told him the facts.

By now it was around midnight, but I felt that I must get to know some more definite information on where we should report, we could waste time wandering round Paris. It occurred to me that although the U. S. Air Force was moving out, the Army might still be in occupation.

The building we were in was used normally as a college, and in the hall I found a telephone. I entered into a long conversation with the operator on the Paris Exchange. This got me connected to the Adjutant of the Officer Commanding (Paris Area) who knew all about evaders, and he gave me directions to the special hotel where we were to assemble. Despite the late hour he was very helpful, and said that there were about 30 men a day coming into Paris. One up for the brown jobs.

We found the hotel next morning and it was wonderful, (Hotel Meurice) excellent accommodation, soft beds and a change of clothes. We were issued with superb American khaki shirts and trousers and the R. A. F. Officer in charge advanced us £5 Sterling as spending money! This was a small fortune in recently liberated Paris, and we enjoyed our stay for a couple of days, whilst the flight back home was arranged. Albert and I went out one evening and finished up at a very high class establishment, where we used the £5 in the best possible way in Paris.

We were still a mysterious looking bunch wandering round the bars in Paris, for our khaki outfits had no markings, regimental or Air Force; luckily we were not picked up by the M. P.s.

My flight back to Hendon from Paris was in a Dakota, which flew daily, carrying the Kings Messenger. The date was September 17th 1944, the same day that the battle for Arnheim started. After a de-briefing in London at the Marylebone Hotel (M. I. 9 H. Q.) I returned to my home in Pinner. I 'phoned ahead from the Railway Station to let my Mother and eldest brother get over the shock, I guessed they would only have had the bad news of my disappearance.

My actual return home was very emotional.

I found the telegram to my Mother announcing my non return from Wesseling, a spine chilling message, and the follow up letters from the Commanding Officer of the Squadron and the Padre both very sympathetic. These had been followed by my personal effects, returned from East Kirkby, not a lot of consolation for a bereaved relative. My Mother had been badgering the Red Cross for news, and had received a letter from them to say that four of our crew -Taffy Raffill (Rear Gunner) Alan Applegath (mid-upper Gunner) Lofty Hydes (Wireless Operator) and Vie Spalding (Navigator) were Prisoners of War, but there was no news of the other three members of the crew.

A telegram to my Mother from Air Ministry announced my safe return, but I had got home before it. I was also advised that Joe Hatter, our Flight Engineer, had evaded capture and returned home via Brussels. That left only our pilot "Ginger" Guy unaccounted for, I was concerned as to his fate. When I had first met Madame Janssen I enquired whether she was aware of any other aircrew landing in the area of Eisden, and she had told me that one body was in a local Church. She could not get a name, because the Germans were on guard, but the description she gave, especially quoting the red hair, sounded like our pilot There were many crashed aircraft at the time, and I had been hoping that Ginger had survived; now we were all accounted for, except him.

Abingdon Oxford

I was sent on "survivor's leave" with extra food ration coupons to get my strength back, although my Belgian helpers had not let me starve. During this leave I returned to my old Squadron at East Kirkby, where I met the C.O. W/Cdr Humphries.

He was very interested to hear that we had been shot down by flak, most of the losses on the Wesseling raid had been due to German fighters. The losses were 27% of the total aircraft involved. East Kirkby lost 12 aircraft and closed for a period while news crews and aircraft were posted in. I made some enquiries about the crews who had been operating at the same time as us, and found that only one had finished their tour. Even they had been finished at 29 trips, because the crew had suffered two aircraft so badly damaged that they were scrapped, one mid-upper gunner killed and one ditching in the North Sea!

I visited my old billet on a site above the airfield and found my 'bike, more or less where I had left it 3 months before. An A.c.2 batman had found it and used it, no doubt hoping that no-one would ever claim it. He should have handed it in to the 'Committee of Adjustment' who dealt with the effects of missing aircrew, but he had looked after it, so I settled for him to put it on the train to my home address.

Whilst near Boston I called on Iris to see if she had missed me, or whether she remembered me from the few weeks I had known her. She seemed pleased to see me, but put things in perspective, by saying that over the War years she had met several aircrew who had gone missing. She had indeed 'phoned the Officers Mess and when told that I was not available put two and two together from her previous experience. So much for romance!

She said, also, that since I had disappeared, she had met some Airborne lads , who had moved into the area, but they had gone off to Arnheim. (Not many of them came back)

I was summoned to Air Ministry for an interview to decide what I should do next. It seemed obvious to me that I should re-join my squadron, after all, that is what I had been trying to do from the time I was shot down.

The Officer who interviewed me seemed evasive, as though rejoining my unit might cause difficulties, or perhaps he had some laid down procedure for evading aircrew. (He was indeed sticking to the rules, I did not know, but some earlier evaders, on returning to their squadrons had given details of their helpers to their friends. Subsequently when some of these were shot down, the details got to the Gestapo, the helpers were rounded up and shot. It had been decided to keep returning evaders off ops for at least 6 months.) The advance of Allied troops had liberated a good part of France and Belgium, so that did not really apply to me, but he was playing by the book.

When I received my posting, some two weeks later, it was to an O. T. U. (Operational Training Unit). In effect, this was putting me back six months, and meant crewing up again with a completely new crew. I reported to Abingdon with a sense of anti-climax, definitely cheesed off.

The situation got worse, when I discovered that the crews from Abingdon eventually finished up flying Halifaxes from Squadrons based in Yorkshire. Whilst I had no doubt the Halifax boys did a good job, I decided that I must try to get back on ops in my old Group(5) as soon as possible.

I tried "normal" channels at first and asked the Adjutant for an interview with the Wing Commander in charge of the O. T. U. On learning the object of my interview (i.e. getting posted!), the Adjutant said that there was no chance, and that I was wasting my time. He recommended that I accept the situation as it was, and I got the impression that I should not waste his time either.

The crewing up process had gone on meantime, and I was part of a new crew, of which only one other member had flown on ops. The pilot had recognised me, for during his spell in between tours of ops, he had been flying Ansons at Staverton giving us experience of conditions in England, after our training in South Africa. He was now going on to his second tour and had been pleased to find somebody else who had flown on ops, for his new crew.

It needed some drastic action on my part to get things altered, and the opportunity came for me in the Officers Mess one lunch-time. Abingdon was a Base unit and had a fair proportion of high-ranking officers using the Mess. Among them was an Air Vice Marshal, who must have been somewhat wary of the Flying Officer who accosted him in the corner of the Mess, when he was about to drink his coffee after lunch.

He listened patiently to my tale of frustration at being at an O.T.U. when I wanted to rejoin my Squadron on ops, and said that he would see what he could do although he was making no promises.

The adjutant sent for me the next day; "the Wing Commander wants to see you", he said. I was duly wheeled in to see the Wingco who said dryly "that he had been told that I wanted to return to an operational squadron immediately" I explained that I had gone to some trouble to get back to this country, and that it was wasting time to train me yet again, could I not return to my old squadron?

He was obviously sympathetic to my request, not only because of the Air Vice Marshal I felt ,but because he knew what operational flying was all about, for he had a row of medal ribbons, including the D.F.C. My interview finished with his assurance that I would be posted as soon as possible. The adjutant remarked to me as I left his office "You're lucky, I would never have given you a dog's chance of a posting". Perhaps he didn't take coffee in the Mess!

I was sent on leave from Abingdon over the period of Christmas 1944, pending a posting to an operational squadron in 5 Group; not my original 57 Squadron, but a specialist squadron in the same Group - No. 9.

Bardney

I arrived at Bardney in Lincolnshire early on the morning of 1st January 1945. Number 9 Squadron were the sole occupants, at that time, of this Nissen-hutted camp. I was amazed to find crashed aircraft littered across the airfield, one, just yards off the road where I passed. I learned later that these aircraft had been part of a sortie directed against the Dortmund Ems canal, ice on the aircraft and runway had caused havoc on take off, two having crashed. There had been several fatalities, one rear gunner had crawled from his burning aircraft and escaped along the ditch beside the road. (Welcome back, I thought)

I had been posted to Bardney as a replacement for a Canadian Air Bomber, Jack Singer, who was returning to Canada when he finished his first tour of operations (30 sorties). He and his crew had two more ops to go, and the others had chosen to go on for a second tour, immediately following the first.

Crews had the option after 30 sorties of a break, as Instructors on training units, before returning to ops. There was no guarantee, however, that they would be able to return as a crew, in addition, the advantage of going straight on meant the reduction to only a further 20 sorties to complete the second tour.

I was introduced to the crew which, apart from Jack the Canadian Air Bomber, consisted of Doug Tweddle pilot, Edward Shields, nicknamed 'Cas' as Navigator, Charlie Heath -Flight Engineer, Alan Foot - mid-upper gunner, Ken Mallinson -rear gunner and Paddy Carson - Wireless Operator. They had started their tour of Operations in August 1944, whilst I was in Belgium, and had become one of the experienced crews specialising in the use of the "Tallboy" 12000 pound bomb.

This bomb had been designed by Barnes Wallis and had a super sleek shape which reduced drag. On impact it would penetrate concrete fortifications, when dropped in the vicinity of a target, such as a bridge, it produced a blast and was christened "the earthquake bomb". In order to get the best results of penetration it meant that the Tallboy had to be

116

Flt/Lt Doug Tweddle 9 Squadron
(he was adamant that his bomb sank the Tirpitz in November 1944)

dropped from over 8000' which also avoided possible blast damage to the attacking aircraft itself; hence the need for experienced crews who could bomb accurately.

9 Squadron, along with 617, had attacked various targets in daylight with this bomb, U-boat pens, V1 rocket sites and the most spectacular,

had sunk the Tirpitz in its Norwegian fjord hideout. They were now being switched to attack German supply routes, strategic bridges, railways and viaducts, as a separate unit of Bomber Command.

Instead of saturation bombing at night, with hundreds of aircraft carrying 1000lb bombs and incendiaries, a small number of aircraft (10-15) carrying the Tallboy, were to make precision attacks in daylight.

There was a tremendous spirit on the Squadron and I was soon absorbed and made part of it, to them I was to be Doug Tweddle's new Bomb Aimer and nobody asked or worried what I had been up to before. Most of the crews had had some "hairy" experiences, the wireless operator of one, George Thompson, had just been awarded the V.C., posthumously. He has been on the trip to the Dortmund Elms canal the day I arrived at Bardney.

There was no discussion about these experiences, except perhaps in a reference to a humorous incident. Crews that had gone missing were said to "have got the chop" or "gone for a Burton", no further comment was necessary.

I was soon flying practice-bombing flights with Doug Tweddle and his crew, waiting for them to complete their two ops, so that I could take over from Jack Singer when he left for Canada. Nothing was said, but obviously I was being "vetted" for suitability; I think the C.O. of the Squadron, Wing Commander Bazin and the Bombing Leader Bill Campbell, an Australian, were concerned that I might be "twitchy".

Bill approached me in the Mess, quite informally, "Do you think you'll be O.K. sport?" he said "how soon do you want to operate again?" "What a gentleman" I thought, until it transpired that another crew had an Air Bomber off sick, and Bill wanted me to go in his place. The Bombing Leader had found use for the "spare bod".

The next two days I was airborne with Flying Officer Mackintosh and his crew on practice bombing and fighter affiliation; they were checking me out as well! The third day I went on my first daylight raid to Altenbeken viaduct, 17 aircraft from 9 Squadron carrying 12000lb Tallboys.

One of the differences I found between night and day bombing was that in daylight, the flak appeared as black puffs of smoke in the sky, instead of bright twinkles of light. Somehow, the smoke seemed more ominous because it hung in the sky, and if it was ahead one realised that trouble was hanging there, waiting for us to fly in.

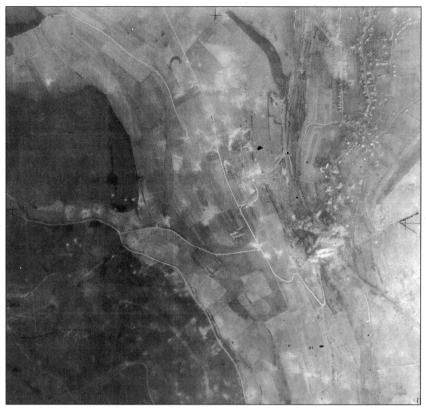

Altenbeken Viaduct 22.2.45 - Bomb bursting on target

Much appreciated, however, were the fighter escorts, usually 50 aircraft; they kept well clear of us, after all we were being shot at, but their controller on the Radiotelephone (R.T.) was in contact with our Bomber Leader, we knew they were in the close vicinity, and felt protected.

There had been the occasion, however, only a fortnight earlier when the Squadron had been on an attack in Norway, that the protection slipped. The fighter escort had seen some German aircraft on the ground and attacked these leaving the bombers unprotected. The latter had' then been jumped by German fighters and lost several aircraft; the sequel being a personal apology from the C.O. of the fighter squadron, some more mad impetuous Poles.

Another aspect of daylight bombing was the ability to see and identify the target at some distance, and to be able to release the Tallboy and watch it dropping clown towards the target, finally bursting with a great impact. Altenbeken viaduct was demolished.

119

Frank Hawkins (Armourer) with Tallboy 12000 Pound Bomb (Photo courtesy Frank Hawkins)

Within two days I was off again with F/O Mackintosh, this time to the infamous Dortmund Ems Canal, which was attacked regularly throughout the War, in an effort to keep it drained. There was one section where the canal crossed the River Ems by aqueduct and. was vulnerable to concentrated attack. The problem was, of course, that the heaviest defences were grouped around this point, so every attack was in for trouble.

On this sortie the Met boys got it wrong, when we arrived over the Dortrnund area, there was an unbroken layer of cloud beneath us stretching as far as the eye could see. Since the height of the cloud base was no more than 3000' we could not bomb with Tallboys, so we had to return to Bardney, bringing the bombs with us. They were too few and precious to drop off anywhere!

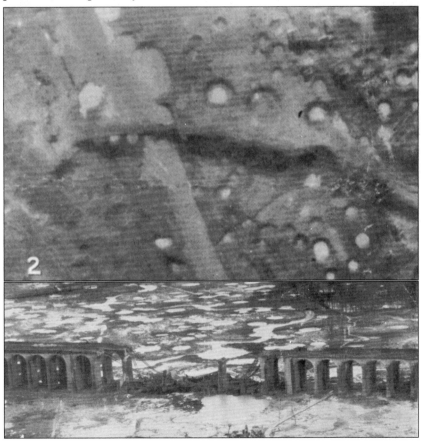

Attacks on bridges and viaducts in March 1944 (Top: Arnsberg Rail Bridge, Above: Bielefeld viaduct)

The old car, that my former crew had left on the dispersal point at East Kirkby the night we had gone missing, had disappeared by the time I returned 3 months later. There was a laid down procedure for crews personal equipment and transport for use whilst they were on ops. It involved registering the items with a "Committee of Adjustment" which body had the sad job of getting missing crews' effects together and sending them back to the next of kin. With a car owned jointly by several crew members, they would auction it off, and divide the money equally to the next of kin.

It relied on crews registering their possessions; but we had not bothered with our old banger. Like many others, whilst not superstitious of course, to register with the "C of A" was tempting fate. It couldn't happen to us unfortunately, it did. With the back pay that had accrued whilst I was in Belgium, I bought an old Morris 8, and had a new engine put in it, all for less than £100!

We, Doug Tweddle's crew, found it very useful. Bardney was truly the site of the ditty often sung in the Mess - "We come from Bardney, a--- ---e of the World and all the Universe". The village itself did not deserve such derogation, the locals were truly hospitable, and the pubs a second home to us

The snag was the distance from Bardney to anywhere else. Lincoln, the nearest town of any size was 15 miles away, out of bicycle range, and Boston, in the other direction, 25 miles away. With the car, on "Stand down" from ops, we could get to such sinful places as Nottingham, blowing all my petrol coupons in one wild orgy.

My third op, the first with Doug Tweddle, was to Arnsberg Bridge, some distance beyond Dortmund, but this time again the cloud obscured the target. To make matters worse, as we turned for home, one engine developed a fault so that we had to reduce speed, and limp back behind the rest of the Squadron. Landing with the Tallboy on board, and only three engines was normally not too difficult, but the thick cloud over the target had spread back to our base in the form of fog by the time we reached England.

The controller in the Watchtower at Bardney suggested we land at nearby Waddington, where perhaps the visibility was better; it wasn't, of course, being only 15 miles away. We made two attempts to land at Waddington, during which we all had a very close look at a very large hanger, which appeared when we expected to see a runway.

I think thr Flying Control at Waddington took exception to us trying to demolish their hanger, and possibly some of the airfield for it was suggested then, that we flew to Carnaby in Yorkshire, where the visibility was better and the runway very long indeed, with Fog Intensive Disposal Of (F.I.D.O.) facilities as well.

There were three such airfields, with special long runways for damaged bombers returning without brakes, faulty hydraulics or generally shot to pieces. Carnaby (Yorks), Manston (Kent), Woodbridge (Suffolk). We landed safely at Carnaby, and left the aircraft to the ground Engineers to sort out the trouble overnight.

We went to temporary billets nearby, with some sleeping accommodation, which consisted of several rows of bunks lining the big Nissen huts. One just found a convenient bunk, preferably unoccupied, and turned in. I mention this, because we had barely got our heads down before a whole crowd of aircrew came in from rival 617 Squadron. They had been diverted from their base at Scampton, which had completely closed due to the fog. "Where are those 'buggers' from 9 Squadron?" they shouted, a coarse lot indeed; they never could get over the fact that 9 Squadron sank the Tirpitz, not them.

Fortunately for us, there were several other crews spread among the bunks, so we kept quiet and let the shouting wash over us. They settled down at last, and threw lumps of coal at the light bulb to extinguish it; they were not very accurate at that either, but persevered until the bulb was shattered.

Next morning, we were assured that our faulty engine had been repaired, so we taxied out and took off for return to Bardney. We had barely reached flying speed when the same engine failed again, and take off on three engines, with a Tallboy, is not to be recommended. We made it, however, and landed at Base where we were met by the Engineering Officer, anxious to find out why we were still flying around on three engines with a bomb load. On being made aware of the circumstances, he turned a bright crimson with rage, and headed off by car to Yorkshire, breathing fire and slaughter.

Two days later, we went back for Arnsberg Bridge and this time in good visibility, we hit it from 12000'. Not without opposition or loss, however, for on the way to the target one of our formation was hit by flak, caught fire, and sank lower and lower. We all watched and counted the parachutes as the crew jumped, only five out of the seven made it, before the plane hit the ground and exploded.

I am sure that the feeling of all the crews that watched and counted, was not one of how lucky they were not to be in that crashing aircraft, but a willing for the crew to get out, and a sense of sadness for the loss of friends who they could not help.

On the return journey, another aircraft reported engine trouble; the aircraft itself was shaking like a leaf and the pilot ordered the crew to jump, expecting pieces to fall off at any moment. He decided to hold on as long as possible, together with the Flight Engineer, and we were detailed to accompany him to the nearest airfield for an emergency landing, which turned out to be Charleroi in Belgium.

The rest of the crew, who had baled out, were over German occupied territory, and I met the Air Bomber some weeks later. He had regained our lines successfully and was a little put out to find that he need not have jumped after all.

We were delayed at Charleroi for two days, pinned down by poor weather, and when we flew back to Bardney we brought the crewless pilot and flight engineer with us, their own aircraft needed an engine replacement. A few days later we were surprised when a very smart young lady of the Air Transport Auxiliary flew the aircraft back to Bardney.

Meanwhile we attacked another bridge at Vlotho on the Weser between Osnabruck and Hanover, my fifth daylight op, and as a crew, we were now selected for the important job of' wind finding for the main formation.

It entailed breaking away from the other aircraft in the vicinity of the target, and flying a special triangular course which our Navigator, Cas Shields, plotted on his chart. From this plot he could deduce an accurate wind speed and direction for setting on the bombsight, thus ensuring we got the best possible information in the target area.

There would be, three aircraft out of fifteen involved in the attack, which would find these target winds, pass them to the Leader, and then rejoin for the attack. He would assess these and give the result to all the bombing force. One felt isolated, flying about Germany in daylight obtaining this information, the accompanying fighters having all disappeared as we neared the target. Only the Leader was in R/T touch with the fighters all the time, so that although we assumed they were around, we could neither hear nor see them.

The railway bridge at Vlotho was left with a lop-sided look about it, and useless as a river crossing.

During this period, mid-February 1945 - March 1945, the purpose of our bombing was to swamp the rapid repair service set up by the Germans, whenever their road or rail links to the Ruhr were broken. Using foreign and P.O.W. labour they had maintained an efficient repair service; our precise bombing of the viaducts at Altenbeken, Bielefeld (helped by 617) and Arnsberg cut the three most important rail routes. The Bielefeld viaduct survived several attacks before we visited it in the company of some aircraft of 617 carrying the 'Grand Slam' 22000lb bomb.

There was also an aircraft from the Photo Unit which took the well known picture of the big bomb just as it was dropped. This was fine, but they kept the rest of us circling round the target, while they took some more film, presumably in case the first lot did not come out!

In between our trips to Germany, we were kept at practice on the bombing range at Epperstone, near Nottingham, just to keep our eye in I suppose; the unofficial motto of the Squadron was most appropriate "There's always bloody something".

This motto was emblazoned on a board in the Mess, with every sortie that 9 Squadron had carried out since 1939. The motto originated from a quote by G/Cpt Pickard, early in the war, when he was a member of 9 sqdn; later he lost his life in a daring raid on Amiens jail, flying a Mosquito in a low level attack.

V.E. day and after

When off duty we visited the local pub in Bardney- The Jolly Sailor- and returning to the Officer's Mess late one night, we could hear shouts of laughter, as we approached. This was not unusual, as those officers who did not go out, assembled in the Mess for drinking sessions with much 'line-shooting', which became more extravagant as the evening went on. Puzzling, however, were the short periods of silence, between hysterical laughter. As we entered through the blackout curtains, the room was plunged into darkness. 'NOW' said a voice, and a match was struck, followed by a vivid blue flame, about 3 feet off the floor, and two feet in length. The lights came on to reveal one man stretched face down over the back of a chair, with another person at his rear end, poised with matches at the ready. It transpired that the silent periods were for the consumption of a tankard of Guinness, and the gas to be pressurised internally, to be released at the precise moment of striking the match. Jet propulsion in its infancy!

On my 6th op with Doug Tweddle, we were scheduled to attack Bremen harbour, and the U Boat pens, but had only been airborne a short while before an engine went unserviceable (u/s) and we had to turn back, since we could not maintain formation with a full bomb and petrol load.

The next day, however, op number seven, we were despatched as lead aircraft in a formation of nine bombers and forty-five fighters to attack a railway bridge over the Weser at Bad Oeynhausen not very far from our last target at Vlotho.

It was one of those days in March, there is usually only one, when the weather was perfect; not a cloud in the sky, warm enough to walk out without a coat, just a light breeze. Perfect, and ideal bombing weather too.

The flight to within fifteen minutes from the target was uneventful, the fighter escort appeared, flew with us, then retired to a safe distance. We flew the special course to ascertain the wind speed and direction and were

126

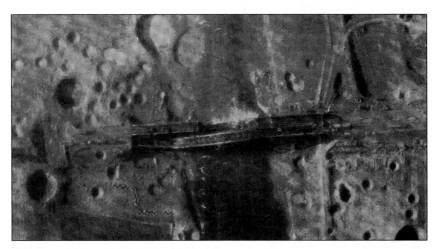

The railway bridge at Bad Oynhausen the day after our attack
(It was not only towns like Dresden that were attacked at this stage of the war - these targets were specifically requested by the army to stop German troops and supplies reaching the forward areas)

Ground crew with 'Y' Yoke (The aircraft that returned safely after being peppered by flak over Bad Oynhausen

amazed to find that the wind speed was nearly zero. Two other aircraft confirmed this, and we lined up for the target all nine in file, each aircraft aiming and dropping it's Tallboy independently. Although we were the lead aircraft, each of the others made their own attack.

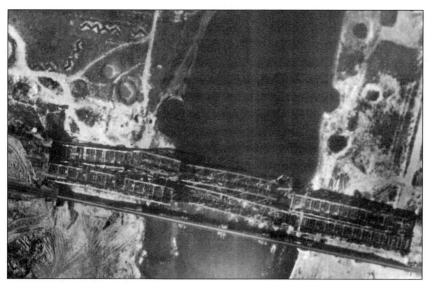

The Railway Bridge at Bad Oynhausen (plus emergency pipe line installed 1945)

The flak started up ahead, and it was very heavy, they knew our target, there were not many bridges left ! The day was so clear, I could see our destination in the distance, plenty of time to check over the bombsight settings and ask Doug Tweddle to open the bomb doors. This altered, slightly, the flying trim of the aircraft and was normally done early in the run up, for the pilot to get the plane settled back to the correct speed and direction of approach.

A flick of the switch set the bomb release for a live drop, just the word "right" or "left, left" was enough to get Doug Tweddle to make small corrections to ensure we were aiming true. The bombsight assimilated all the necessary information (including aircraft height and speed, wind direction and speed (as given by our wind-finding manoeuvre) and supplied the correct release point to me.

This was done by means of a light, most appropriately in the shape of a sword, superimposed on a small glass panel, through which one observed the target. With the point of the sword directed through the aiming point, the release time for the bomb was when the target reached the crosspiece or hilt of the sword. The glass was kept level, during any banking turn by a gyroscope.

Bomb release was operated by pushing with the thumb on a hand held switch, the bombing tit. On this particular day, I was, as usual, concentrating on the run up to the target, trying to ignore the thumps and black puffs of the flak.

It must have been worse for the other crewmembers, Doug Tweddle and I had something to concentrate on. As Leader we were "listening out" also, for any information from the fighter escort , and that channel suddenly burst into life. There came a frantic chatter from the Fighter Controller, not that we could see or do much as we were on a committed bombing run.

The bridge slid under the sword, "Bomb gone" I said, (always a welcome from the rest of' the crew for that,) and the aircraft lifted as the weight left the bomb bay. "Bomb doors closed" I requested Doug Tweddle, and watched the Tallboy drop down to explode alongside the bridge.

At that moment there was a deep thump, and a crack like a rifle shot echoed through the aircraft. The Flight Engineer's reaction was to fling himself down on the floor, at the same time pushing all the throttles wide open, so that the engines roared at full revs. He was giving Doug Tweddle full power, assuming we were under attack by fighters.

We had been hit, not by fighters, but by flak, which had peppered us in several places; the loud crack was the Perspex canopy above the pilot being penetrated, but the more severe damage we discovered later.

The chatter from the Fighter Controller was next explained, as the last aircraft of our flight reported that he had been attacked by a M.E. 262 jet fighter on his bombing run. He had taken avoiding action and had only slight damage to the tail fin of the aircraft; unfortunately he had been forced to jettison his Tallboy. The German jet, being much faster than our escort, had dived from above our formation, attacked the last aircraft and continued on and away before our fighters could get near him.

Our own damage now became apparent, for on testing that the undercarriage was not damaged, (by lowering it) it refused to come up again; the hydraulic system had been fractured. In addition, the aircraft behind us reported streams of vapour coming from under our wings.

Our return to Base was slow, with the wheels down, not quite sure whether the vapour was hydraulic fluid leaking away, or petrol from the main tanks in the wings, which could ignite at any moment.

I was spared having to "hit the silk" again, however, we landed safely at Bardney, and after taxying on to the dispersal we climbed out to see the damage. The vapour was indeed petrol, the self-sealing tanks in the wing had been punctured and the petrol poured out in a steady stream on to the tarmac as we stood there.

I walked round to the front of the aircraft and looked up at my bomb-aimer's viewing panel - there was a hole drilled straight through it, on the opposite side of the bombsight from where I had looked down at the target.

The results of the bombing, as shown on the reconnaissance photo taken by a special Mosquito, were excellent. The bridge was destroyed, with both tracks fallen into the river; with only eight effective bombs; we could justifiably claim it as the "classiest little prang in 5 Group".

It turned out that we had made our last operational sortie of the European war, for after a few days of practice bombing and cross-country flights, we were off on leave. On our return we found that we had missed the last Tallboy sortie, which was to the "Wolf's Lair" at Berchtesgarten, and that an Armistice had been signed to end the European War on 8th May 1945.

On VE Day itself an aircraft from the Squadron had flown over Central London, with Richard Dimbleby on board; to give his impression of the celebrations from above. Unfortunately there was thick cloud down to a low level, and any commentary must have been inspired guesswork.

Japan remained, however, and practice bombing continued; we had an added interest in flying to France and Belgium to bring back released P.O.W.'s. Each flight we carried 24 ex P.O.W. and despite the fact that there was little comfort for them, they were pleased to be getting back home. They had to squat down on the metal floor in the fuselage of the Lancaster, the noise and motion must have put many of them off flying for life. After some years in a prison camp, however, they were prepared to endure anything, and I used to get the map out and show them where we were as we flew back.

It was an emotional moment for them to see the white cliffs and coastline, and there were many moist eyes, including ours, as we touched down at Dunsfold, where we left them before returning to Bardney.

There were some casualties even so, on one occasion as the Lancaster made its approach to land, one of the ex P.O.W.' passengers stood up, and to steady himself grabbed at the dinghy release handle and pulled it. This caused the dinghy to inflate from its storage in the upper wing surface, resulting in the crash of the aircraft with loss of crew and passengers.

Having the car, and being fairly mobile, I took the opportunity when we were 'stood down' of calling on Iris in Boston. She accepted that I might have a chance of survival, so we became engaged. I often gave a lift to another crew member on a similar visit to his girl friend; he had a useful contact with a farmer and his family on the outskirts of Boston. They were very hospitable, and put on a meal for us whenever we called, but we had to endure some earthy humour, as to the purpose of our journey. After a meal of bacon and eggs etc. (both rationed for the majority) they would send us on our way with such remarks as 'that will put blood in your pencil'.

At the end of May 1945, 9 Squadron were allocated to "Tiger Force" with other squadrons and sent off to India en route for the Japanese theatre of war.

We, as a crew, were deemed to have done enough for the time being, and were posted to 50 Squadron at Sturgate near Gainsborough. Here we continued with the bombing exercises, night cross-countries, fighter affiliation and a most interesting photo reconnaissance trip over many of the German towns reduced to rubble. In most of these there was not a house left standing slum clearance on a grand scale; the occupants had only one option, clear it and rebuild it, which they did with a certain amount of assistance from America.

On this flight we took several ground crews to let them see what we had been up to. A kind of 'Cook's Tour of the Ruhr.

In August we started ferrying troops from Italy, bringing them home for leave or demobilisation. We flew out to Pomigliano near Naples, collected 20 passengers, plus their luggage, and returned to Glatton, near Peterborough, where the Customs were established. Our bomb bays were equipped with hessian panniers to stow the baggage, mostly kit bags, and the flight took seven hours each way. We would fly out one day, stay the next in Italy, and return to Glatton on the third, off-load the passengers, and fly the short distance back to our base at Sturgate.

It was a long tiring journey and with the summer storms over Northern Italy quite exciting; not to mention dangerous, but we enjoyed the middle day at Naples. We became adept at haggling in the local markets and bargained for cameos and trinkets; we saw the beauties of Sorrento, including those on the beach, who refused flatly to even talk to us.

We visited Pompeii and were shown the sign of good luck, and for a couple of cigarettes we were given a grand tour of the artistic murals. Our most enjoyable visits were to the San Carlo opera; the atmosphere of an Italian audience participating in an opera has to be experienced, there is something tangible about it, as though they are willing the singers to produce their best.

If that was not forthcoming there were shouts and groans, even for the leading named principals of the performance. The last act, however, usually seemed to be perfect and to everybody's satisfaction, so the audience left happy. We were a little shaken at first by loud cries of "bis" during the performance, which sounded derogatory, but turned out to be "encore" in their language. It was all before the days of English National Opera, we just enjoyed the music and singing, and worked out the plot as best we could.

Apart from the main street in Naples - via Roma - all the others were marked OFF LIMITS, whether to protect the large number of Americans wandering about, or the locals from the soldiery, I never knew. On the main street we were accosted on all sides by small boys offering us cigarettes, decorative postcards and their sisters. They would also change pound notes into Lire, at a very good rate of exchange, and this meant going with them down the "off limit" side streets. If we had given them the pounds and waited for them to come back, we would never have seen them again.

On one of these banking trips, I collected the pounds from the crew, set off with a small urchin and dived in and out of' alleys and back streets, arriving eventually at a second floor flat. I exchanged the money, after the necessary haggle over the rate, and started on my way back, keeping a wary eye open for trouble. I was glad to see Doug Tweddle and the Flight Engineer, Jimmy Robe, coming to look for me. I think they were concerned for my personal safety, or it could just have been that I was carrying all the money!

We averaged two trips a month from August to December 1945 to Italy, interspersed with training flights. In January 1946 we were sent to Berlin, one of the last crews to participate in "Operation Spasm".

This was a sightseeing visit which had operated on a daily basis since the previous August; Lancasters Halifaxes and Stirlings had flown into Gatow airfield, Berlin, for their crews to take a look at the city they had attacked so often, and to take back troops on leave, as we had done from Italy.

A specially fitted truck was made available to take us from the airfield into Berlin, and we visited the Chancellery and Hitler's bunker. Under the gaze of the Russian sentry we examined the spot where Hitler's body had been soaked in petrol and set on fire, and although the War had been over since the previous May, the devastation was complete.

The Russian zone in particular was littered with the debris of the fighting, burnt out tanks, derelict and bullet marked buildings. Most poignant were the German steel helmets littered all around; had their owners flung them down at the moment of surrender?, or were they just tossed aside as the bodies were collected for burial? Mostly the latter, I thought, for the Russians had a score to settle.

On the lighter side, we went to an Officer's club for a meal, paid for in cigarettes, which were still the most popular currency. The meal itself was typically English, roast beef etc., superbly cooked and the cigarettes ensured we had first class service from the German waiters. With a bottle of champagne to round it off, we felt that perhaps we had won the war after all.

Before leaving Berlin, we bartered some more cigarettes for cut glass bowls, vases and glasses and Doug Tweddle was advised to keep to some very strict rules for take-off and especially landing, with all that valuable glass aboard.

In February, 50 Squadron moved from the spartan Nissen huts at Sturgate to the permanent station at Waddington, demobilisation gathered pace and as the war experienced veterans left, another form of veteran took over.

These were permanent commissioned officers, many of whom seemed to have missed the action in far off places, but they remembered the R.A.F. as it had been, before the conscripts ruined it.

From the days of the Fighter pilots with scarf and top tunic button undone, to the Bomber boy (with his officer's hat grease stained and bent down each side like spaniels' ears) standards of discipline and uniform had deteriorated. The impact, however, of these returning expatriates was considerable; Applications for Permanent Commissions fell to zero, "roll on demob", was the cry!

At the training level, the long distance flights and bombing practice were given official code names, and the routes we flew were designated with a letter of the alphabet. On the squadron itself, daily parades at 8a.m. were re-imposed and the new Adjutant endeared himself to me, by putting me on to taking statements from all concerned in the proposed court martial of an officer who had lost his revolver. I was so successful at this, that the Adjutant tried to get me for yet another Court Martial; I declined, politely, my demob day was the following week.

I left Waddington on 8th July 1946 as a Flight Lieutenant, heading for Uxbridge demob. centre, four years and five months after joining up at Lords cricket ground. I felt I was leaving a way of life and security for the unknown; most of my friends, however, had already been demobbed,

Jimmy Robe (Flight Engineer) Doug Tweddle (Pilot) Doug Jennings (Bomb Aimer) (After a hazardous sortie in the back streets of Naples)

50 Squadron Aircraft lined up on Tarmac at Gatow Berlin

BERLIN AIR LINE

PRODUCED AND PUBLISHED BY R.A.F. GATOW

NO. 11   FRIDAY, JANUARY 25th 1946   1 MARK

U.N.O. FACING FIRST TEST

U.S. Urges Postponement

FOLLOWING THE SUBMISSION BY PERSIA OF HER CASE TO THE SECURITY COUNCIL OF U.N.O. AND THE SOVIET UNION'S REQUEST THAT THE INDONESIAN AND GREEK SITUATIONS ALSO BE INVESTIGATED, AMERICAN DELEGATES, LED BY MR. BYRNES, HAVE DECLARED THEMSELVES IN FAVOUR OF POSTPONING THESE CONSIDERATIONS UNTIL APRIL, WHEN U.N.O. IS DUE TO MEET IN THE UNITED STATES FOR THE SECOND PART OF ITS DELIBERATIONS.

The American statement, that the machinery of U.N.O. is not yet properly completed, or sufficiently strong to take the strain of such matters, has met little sympathy in some British quarters, where there is a feeling of urgency to put forward Britain's case on Indonesia and Greece at the earliest possible moment.

At the time of going to press it has not been decided when the Council will discuss these questions, but they are regarded as very exacting test cases for a body so newly formed.

Persia, who complains that the Soviet Union is influencing Azerbaijan, her province on the Russian border, in her claim for separation, says she is willing to submit to the closest investigation by members of the Security Council to prove her case.

The Persian delegation, in its Note to the Council, has called its case a "situation" and not a "dispute," which may be of some importance when the question is discussed.

According to Article 77 of the Charter, a party to a "dispute" shall abstain from voting about it in the Security Council. As the matter is a "situation," however, the Soviets can take part in any vote on the application.

As the Big Five must agree in the Security Council on matters other than procedure, it will be interesting to see whether any of these deliberations see firing about a "veto."

MISSION TO JAVA

Sir Archibald Clark Kerr, British Ambassador to Moscow, left by air for Java on Monday where he is to be special representative of the British Government in the Dutch East Indies.

It has been emphasised that Sir Archibald is not going to Batavia in any sense as an arbitrator, but only to help solve a problem. Britain seems to see settled as soon as possible because of the almost daily loss of British lives involved.

STEEL POLICY HITCH

Although the Control Council have announced that the British Government intend to dispossess German mine owners without compensation, a hitch in the decision to be taken regarding steel production in Germany is revealed by Allied authorities.

The British Delegation does not consider this difference mendable, provided that patience and a determination to find agreement are present on all sides. On January 11th, it was announced that

ATOM PLAN APPROVED

After less than two hours discussion —very little of which was devoted to the actual substance of the resolution—the Political and Security Committees of U.N.O. this week approved by 46 votes to none the setting up of a Commission for the control of atomic energy sponsored by the Big Five.

The result means that the resolution certainly one of the most important before the Assembly, will now go forward as it stands, as the Committee's recommendation. With this opportunity for the smaller Powers to express their views on it, or to suggest amendments, has passed.

DEMOB GRIEVANCE

2,000 R.A.F. men staged a "sit-down" strike at Manipur, India, on Wednesday. Slow demobilisation and reduction in air transport home were stated to be their principal grievances.

DELEGATES ON TRUSTEESHIP

In his address to the United Nations Assembly last week, Britain's Foreign Minister, Mr. Ernest Bevin, revealed that Britain had already opened preliminary negotiations for placing Tanganyika, the Cameroons and Togoland under the trusteeship of U.N.O.

He stipulated that the trusteeship would depend on the organisation of satisfactory terms. The administrators, dating back twenty-five years under the League of Nations, would continue until the ultimate objective of self-government or independence was attained. Trusteeship is to be established as a stepping stone to independence in the near future.

With regard to Palestine, Mr. Bevin said that proposals had been deferred pending the findings of the Anglo-American Committee of Inquiry.

GOUIN PREMIER OF FRANCE

De Gaulle Resignation Final

READY TO GO

Top: Last Lancasters of "Operation Spasm" lined up ready for the return trip to Tibenham. Below: The crew and passengers before stepping into their aircraft.

M. FELIX GOUIN, FORMER PRESIDENT OF THE FRENCH ASSEMBLY WHO WAS ELECTED PREMIER BY POPULAR VOTE ON WEDNESDAY IS NOW FORMING HIS CABINET. HE SUCCEEDS GENERAL DE GAULLE WHO RESIGNED AS LEADER OF THE PROVISIONAL GOVERNMENT ON SUNDAY.

De Gaulle's resignation caused a temporary crisis in French affairs, but earlier this week it looked as if the three main parties of the Government might discontinue their collaboration.

However, the Communists eventually withdrew their suggestion of M. Thorez as Premier, in favour of M. Gouin a the Socialist, who is popular with all three parties. The third party of the coalition, the Progressive Catholics, after much discussion and with certain stipulations, also agreed to continue to work in harmony.

Although General de Gaulle gave the cure in military circles as the chief reason for his resignation, it is understood that his dispute with the Communists over the Constitution was one of the main difficulties.

He also stated that he always visualised his task as coming to an end when the National Assembly met and the political parties took over France's destiny, and that he only stayed the extra six months to see the country over the transitional period.

PRESS VISITS SOVIET ZONE

A party of eight correspondents from Britain and the Empire this week completed a seven-day tour of the Russian Zone of Occupation of Germany, where they have been the guests of the Soviet Military Government.

Edmund Townshend, Daily Telegraph Special Correspondent, wrote in despatch that the first impression were of efficient administration at this stage of occupation. He and his colleagues were allowed to question German and Russian officials at all levels.

"Except for the land reform plan under which the Soviet Military Government had broken up big Nazi estates for settlement by small owners, the state is run on lines broadly similar to those administered by the other Allies," he writes.

No attempt was made to prevent the correspondents talking freely with the Germans they met, nor was any request to visit factories, workers' flats or places of entertainment denied.

END OF "SPASM"

"Operation Spasm," the daily R.A.F. Bomber Command shuttle service between Tibenham, in Norfolk, and Gatow air-field, which enabled dozens of bomber crews to see the ruins of Berlin, ended this week.

Since August last year, when the operation began, Lancasters and occasionally Halifaxes and Stirlings, have been a familiar sight at Gatow airfield. Often they stood on fly over the capital and the Berliners became accustomed to seeing them overhead.

After the visiting passengers had disembarked at Gatow it was the practice to specially-fitted three-ton vehicles to take the crews into Berlin, where they were left largely in their own devices. At a late hour the same night the crews would be picked up and taken back to Gatow. Next day the bombers would take off for their return flight to Tibenham, other Lancasters or Halifaxes having started their flight from Tibenham to the German capital meanwhile. Every bomber carried out eight servicing crew, and filled up with as many bare stores and soldiers as possible. In five months approximately 2,000 men ferried in to out of Berlin in this way.

Veto "Blot"

Mr. Frazer, the New Zealand Premier, speaking after M. Gromyko, criticised the Charter for its failure to include in its penalties also the provision against external aggression of the the territorial integrity and political independence of every member of the United Nations and of a pledge to resist such aggression collectively.

"The veto," he said "remains as a blot on the Charter."

M. Bidault, speaking for France, made clear his country's view on the trusteeship of mandated territories.

France we prepared, he said, to ready the terms of an agreement which would define trusteeship for territories under her administration if it were understood that this would not result in weakening the rights of the native population in those territories.

Missing Europeans

M. Bidault also mentioned that it was "remarkable" to see to what degree Europe was absent from the Assembly. "Without Germany, 12 European States representing 130,000,000 people with a

PARLIAMENT RESUMES

Both Houses of Parliament reassembled after the Christmas recess on Tuesday, to settle down to a programme which will offset many aspects of the national life, then have been touched on by any previous peacetime Parliament. Some of the debates may attain historic significance.

With the commencement of the debate on aviation, safety for troops in transit was discussed, and it was revealed that measures such as an increase in the

VYSHINSKY AT GATOW

Air Line newspaper with details of trip to Berlin

the peace time R.A.F. was forming, it was time for me to start again in "civvy" street.

Although, as a schoolboy in 1939, with the coming of the War I had missed the conventional tuition; in the Forces I had been given far broader experiences of life, with a look at other countries and other people. I had survived, where many had not, and I had been very fortunate to find help in Belgium and evade capture.

The members of my crew who became P.O.W's, not only suffered starvation but had to march through snow and ice for many miles as the Germans evacuated their camps ahead of the advancing Russians. To add to their problems they were attacked by 'friendly fighter aircraft'. 'Lofty' Hydes escaped on the march, by hiding and letting the column move on. He joined the local Polish partisans and was liberated by the Russians, who for political reasons delayed his departure home from Odessa.

" Ginger" Guy is buried at Asch (As in Flemish) in Belgium. A small corner of the local church burial ground has been made into a special plot for Ginger and five members of a Wellington crew killed in 1942.

I married Iris in 1946, in the Boston 'Stump'(St. Botolph's Church), and the following year we visited Belgium where we met many of my 'helpers'. We laid a wreath on 'Ginger's grave and amended the mistakes the Germans had made on his metal cross. The War Graves Commission erected a permanent headstone later.

Of my first crew, the Flight Engineer, Joe Hatter, literally parachuted into the back garden of a Resistance member in Eisden, and was moved to Brussels' arriving back in England two days before me .I tried to get him to join me in Bardney, but a Warrant Officer at St Athans, where he was stationed, persuaded him he had done enough.

Vic Spalding (Navigator) was picked up by a German Patrol.

Lofty Hydes,(Wop/Ag) was handed over by the Gendarmes , as was Al Applegath (Mid Upper Gunner).

'Taffy' Raffill(Rear Gunner) had the misfortune to meet a 'ringer', a German dressed as an English airman who had infiltrated the escape line. He promised to help 'Taffy' on his way, and promptly turned him over to the local German troops.

Iris at grave with cross amended (the Germans had used his identity disc as a Sergeant)

Ginger Guy's grave at As (far right) in 1947, other 5 are an Australian crew shot down in a Wellington 1942

Happy Ending

Church at As

Grave with modern headstone -
November 2004

In May 1992 I received a letter from Mr Herman Brulmans, a Belgian Researcher into aircraft crash sites from WW2. The following is an extract from his report:-

The bomber came down in the vicinity of the railway station at As. The Stationmaster was an eye-witness, and went to the crash place, a 500 metres from the railway station, and saw an enormous devastation. A few metres besides the burning wreckage of your airplane he found the body of the pilot. It was a strong man in a well dressed uniform and the body showed no outward wounds. He was found, lying on his back in a little brushwood and grass besides the Bosstraat, direction 'Heiwijk'. When the eye-witness opened his jacket he saw the serious wounds. Then the Germans came and they sent him away with the following words 'Sie haben hier nichts zu suchen.'

The Germans loaded the wreckage on railway carriages for removal.'

Mr Brulmans enclosed a sketch map of the railway station at As on the night of 21/22nd June 1944 made by the Stationmaster, translated into English.

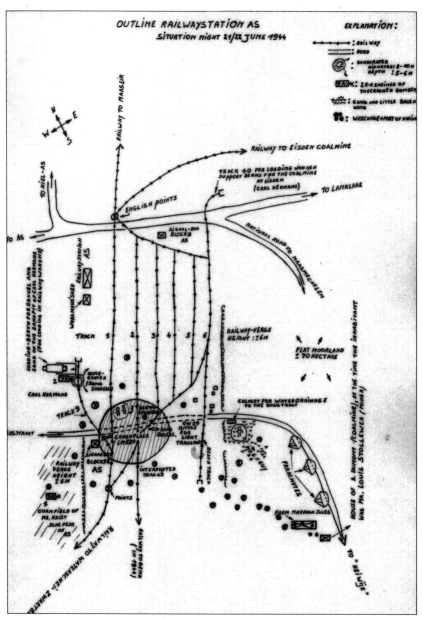

Sketch map of crash site at As